THE TEN COMMANDMENTS FOR TODAY

Walter J. Harrelson

Westminster John Knox Press
LOUISVILLE • LONDON

Book design by Sharon Adams
Cover design by Eric Walljasper, Minneapolis, MN

First edition
Published by Westminster John Knox Press
Louisville, Kentucky

This book is printed on acid-free paper that meets the American National Standards Institute Z39.48 standard. ♾

PRINTED IN THE UNITED STATES OF AMERICA

06 07 08 09 10 11 12 13 14 15 — 10 9 8 7 6 5 4 3 2 1

Library of Congress Cataloging-in-Publication Data
Harrelson, Walter J.
    The Ten commandments for today / Walter Harrelson.—1st ed.
        p. cm.
    Includes bibliographical references.
    ISBN-13: 978-0-664-22931-3 (alk. paper)
    ISBN-10: 0-664-22931-X (alk. paper)
    1. Ten Commandments—Criticism, interpretation, etc.   I. Title.
    BS1285.52.H37   2006
    241.5'2—dc22   200641350

TO OUR GRANDCHILDREN

Heather, Heidi, Ansel, Jessie, Clea, and Tom

Idella and Walter

Contents

Series Introduction

*T*he For Today series is intended to provide reliable and accessible resources for the study of important biblical texts, theological documents, and Christian practices. The series is written by experts who are committed to making the results of their studies available to those with no particular biblical or theological training. The goal is to provide an engaging means to study texts and practices that are familiar to laity in churches. The authors are all committed to the importance of their topics and to communicating the significance of their understandings to a wide audience. The emphasis is not only on what these subjects have meant in the past, but also on their value in the present—"For Today."

Our hope is that the books in this series will find eager readers in churches, particularly in the context of education classes. The authors are educators and pastors who wish to engage church laity in the issues raised by their topics. They seek to provide guidance for learning, for nurture, and for growth in Christian experience.

To enhance the educational usefulness of these volumes, Questions for Discussion are included at the end of each chapter.

We hope the books in this series will be important resources to enhance Christian faith and life.

The Publisher

Preface

*T*he Ten Commandments are in the news today as debates continue over whether they should be posted in public places. The concern behind these debates is serious. Many persons feel that the very foundations of morality are under assault as sweeping changes continue to occur in public manners and morals. Many look for foundations that are permanent and unshakable. That is why religious fundamentalism has gained such ground in many parts of the world today. Even those persons who, in their heart, recognize that their sacred writings have undergone change and development over the centuries will still make for those writings the claim that they are "inerrant and infallible." Small wonder, then, that many individuals and groups call for the public display of the Ten Commandments.

The more important question, however, is what stake do living human beings today have in the content of these ancient words? What help do the commandments offer as we struggle to find our way in an increasingly complex and bewildering moral universe? Are they of any real help?

The premise of this book is that they are still an inadequately mined treasure, a storehouse of wonderfully helpful insight and guidance for the entire population of the earth. Jews and Christians and Muslims share the commandments as part of their religious heritage, but all religions have equivalent moral guidelines that can be compared with the commandments. And the case hardly needs to be made that all persons and all groups need such moral guidelines. Other moral guidelines in society may be rich in meaning and power too; this book is a study of the Ten

Commandments—the riches and power of which have been known by generations. What is their special import for today? That is our question here.

Our plan is to look at the commandments as a collection and also as individual demands. There is much to be learned, of course, from what they meant to ancient Israel and to the religious communities through the centuries. Our chief concern here is what guidance they contain, or may be found to contain, for human beings living on our planet today, facing the issues that the world faces today, confronting moral dilemmas that seem almost overwhelming in their complexity.

Here are some of the questions in my mind as I attempt to speak about the Ten Commandments for today. The list is in no particular order, but it is easy to see how the particular commandments, or some combination of them, might offer illumination.

> How can the goods of earth be shared more equitably among the earth's current population of living beings, and how can these goods best be preserved and passed along to coming generations of living beings?
>
> How can conflicts among human beings be contained and arbitrated?
>
> How can the population of the planet be prevented from outstripping its resources, bearing in mind that ingenuity and new discoveries may enable the planet to support many more millions than one would suppose on the basis of present knowledge?
>
> How can the power of religious belief be drawn on in such a way as not to undercut the very values that most religions espouse?
>
> How can one best account for the apparent longing on the part of most peoples and individuals for transcendent perspectives and meanings—those which insist that the world we know is not self-contained and self-explanatory?
>
> Why is it that so many persons and groups seem never to be content with the life and goods they have? What drives them toward the acquisition of more than their well-being requires?
>
> What accounts for the driving energy of some individuals that will not allow them to rest? And, conversely, why are other individuals perfectly content to do nothing—or no more than circumstances force them to do? What is the source of the

desire to work? And how do we account for the desire to rest and to play?

What are right ways to value life in all its aspects while insisting that physical life itself is not self-explanatory?

What makes sexual attraction and sexual experiences such a mystery to human beings? Does sexual attraction itself constitute one of the defining characteristics of living beings? And is there some distinctive, even unique, element characteristic of *human* sexuality?

What values should human beings place on property? And how can the human community more justly share and enjoy the goods of the earth?

Are there more than pragmatic reasons for truth telling and integrity in public life? How can human beings and groups avoid hurting one another while still honoring the commitment to speak the truth and stand by their words?

Why do so many of us human beings work and struggle for more of earth's goods than we could possibly use? And what is it in us that makes us not only envious of the talents and goods of others but almost sick with envy?

Of course, I do not claim that this study of the Ten Commandments offers adequate answers to such issues and questions. I believe that the commandments do offer concrete assistance as we face these issues. At the least, the exploration might be of use in furthering the debates.

1

Law Is a Gift of God

I am the LORD *your God, who brought you out of the land of Egypt, out of the house of slavery.*
—Exodus 20:2

*T*he quotation above is the beginning of the Ten Commandments. In fact, it is part of the first commandment in the Jewish community to this day. In synagogues and temples, plaques that list the two tables of the Ten Commandments open with the two Hebrew words, *'anoki Adonai,* "I am the LORD." What a great reminder that is for us Christians, that the Jewish community understands law as a gift of God's love and grace! It is true, of course, that the Old Testament lays down many demands that the people of the covenant are to obey, and it is also true that the New Testament emphasizes God's love and grace. But the fact is that for both Testaments and for both communities, God's love and goodness are the setting for God's demands.

We may go even farther. The law is a part of the very structure of the creation. Genesis 1 carefully outlines how God calls the universe into being, building into the good creation its orderly movements and workings, its tasks and responsibilities. God places demands and responsibilities on the earth and its nonhuman creations, just as God requires that human beings populate the earth and exercise responsibility—with God—for its well-being. God's gift of the Ten Commandments to Moses makes explicit what is already implicit in the very structure of the creation. Just as the created universe was a gift of a good

God, so also the words to Moses on the mountain are a good and gracious gift of God.

God's Love in Action

Near the start of the book of Exodus appears these ominous words "Now a new king arose over Egypt, who did not know Joseph." Before long, the plight of Israelites in Egypt had become unbearable. The entire story related in the first fifteen chapters of Exodus contains God's response to the cruel oppression of Israel brought on by this new pharaoh. The struggle takes on cosmic proportions: life itself is threatened by Pharaoh's stubborn refusal to yield to God's demand that the slaves be set at liberty.

Exodus 19:4 sums up this grim history with the words "You have seen what I [the LORD] did to the Egyptians, and how I bore you on eagles' wings and brought you to myself." The whole struggle in Egypt, the plagues, the crossing of the sea, and the trek through the desert—all these were born of God's love and grace. And now, the giving of the Ten Commandments and the other laws completes that act of divine love. Law is a gift of love.

It is a gift of love to Israel, but it is also a gift of love for all the peoples of the world. God reminds Moses, "The whole earth is mine" (Exod. 19:5). Israel is to become "a priestly kingdom and a holy nation" (v. 6), sharing God's gifts and God's demands with "all the families of earth" (see Gen. 12:1–3).

Law in the Ancient Middle East

During the last century and a half, many law collections have been discovered in the Middle East. The most famous is the Code of Hammurabi, king of Babylonia (1792–1750 BCE), but there are also law collections of the Assyrians, the Hittites, and others that have come to light. These law collections have many similarities to the laws found in many parts of the books of Exodus, Leviticus, Numbers, and Deuteronomy. There are no parts of this legislation, however, that very closely resemble the Ten Commandments—in form or in content.

The closest parallels to the demands of the Ten Commandments are lists of curses upon those who would dare to do some terrible deed that threatened the life and welfare of the community. The curse rituals would be read aloud periodically to warn the community against offenses. An early list of such curses, along with a description of the ritual, is found in Deuteronomy 27 and 28. Chapter 28 also lists the blessings that follow from avoidance of these dangerous deeds. The community understood the force of such pronouncements: they were in effect cursing themselves before God—releasing into their world the power of such ominous words and thereby helping them avoid such actions. The swearing of oaths carries the same general sense: "Let X and Y happen to me if I dare to do A or B." And the power of these spoken curses would work even before the community intervened to bring punishment on the maker of an idol (Deut. 27:15) or one who dishonors father or mother (27:16). One who did such a deed would be accursed *already,* even before the community acted—though the community might complete the punishment.

Laws differ in their intended purposes. The majority of legal materials develop over time as the fruit of decisions made by judges or as a result of long-tested experience handed down over the generations. Such laws often take the form, "If X should happen, here is what must be done." This is case law, subject to change over time, of course, as particular cases will have been argued and decided.

Other laws provide the foundation and principles on the basis of which cases are decided. The U.S. Bill of Rights is such a collection, and so is the Universal Declaration of Human Rights, adopted by the United Nations in 1948. The laws of the Bible contain both forms of law, often mixed together. The Ten Commandments are, of course, the second type. This kind of law has been called apodictic or categorical law—that is, law that flatly asserts actions that are not to be undertaken under any circumstances. These categorical laws or law collections may sometimes take the form, "Anyone who does X shall be put to death [or suffer some other severe penalty]." Such laws appear in Exodus 21 and elsewhere in the Bible.

The Ten Commandments are even more basic. They provide no penalties,[1] and thus make clear that these demands are not like those other categorical laws that specify a given punishment. The Ten Commandments are foundational, the groundwork for the laws that are to guide Israel and humankind generally. Over time, explanatory words were added to the commandments to guide the community, it seems; the original form was a set of short, pithy sentences that described actions that would be ruinous for the community and its members and were simply to be avoided. But notice the difference from the curses. Here, the language is not threatening, like that of the curses, but simple and forthright. Each command uses a masculine singular verb, most of them preceded by the negative particle "You shall not," or simply, "Do not." The language is like that of a parent helping the members of the family understand just what sort of family theirs is: "In our family there are some things that we simply do not do." We will use a shortened form of all the commandments as the headings for the next four chapters below.

How the Two Types of Law Functioned

The two types of law have the same end in view: the preservation of the community and its individual members. Some laws have the nonhuman world in view, of course, for God has appointed human beings as stewards of the good earth, charged to do their part in keeping the whole of the creation healthy, passing along to the next generation a viable world for their successors. Some laws make this responsibility for the nonhuman creation explicit. For example, when a town is besieged, the army is not to cut down fruit trees, even for the purpose of erecting platforms from which to attack the enemy. "Are trees in the field human beings that they should come under siege from you?" the text asks (Deut. 20:19–20). The land, similarly, must be preserved from pollution, neglect, or other misuse.

Basically, however, both kinds of law aim at the preservation and welfare of human life. The case laws offer guidance to the elders and judges in the administration of justice. They also exercise restraints on kings or other powerful persons and groups in the community. The prophet Nathan can intervene directly with the king when King David seduces Bathsheba and has her husband killed (2 Sam. 11–12). The prophet Elijah can challenge King Ahab's taking of the vineyard of

Naboth by having Naboth falsely accused of blasphemy and then confiscating his vineyard (1 Kgs. 21).

The categorical kind of law has the same end in view, but it functions differently. This kind of law is not primarily for the elders and judges; it is for everyone, for it embodies the very ethos of the society, its self-understanding, its character. The Ten Commandments would have been taught to the children, memorized—perhaps by reference to the ten fingers, one commandment for each—and recited periodically in religious ceremonies, just as the curses once were recited.

These short prohibitions provide the backbone of Israel's moral life. They say to the community and its individual members, "Whatever else you may do, do not do these prohibited things." To do such things would be a violation of who one was, would be a crime against the God of love who has blessed us in so many ways, would be a crime against our very selfhood. Surely, none in this community will fail to honor their parents! How could anyone dare to use God's name to do harm and violence to a neighbor? Who would actually make an idol? Such things were just "not done in Israel"—an early statement used to denounce dreadful crimes (Gen. 34:7; 2 Sam. 13:12). How could anyone plot to murder a neighbor and carry out the plot? It is not too much to claim, I believe, that without such an understanding of things that simply dare not, must not, be done, any community is in the gravest danger. Every society and all its individuals need to know almost instinctively that there are some things that simply are not done.

The two kinds of commandments supplement each other very well. One type of law is essential for the law courts and all the individuals and institutions that are involved in the administration of justice. The other type of law supports and safeguards the moral life of a people. It helps to define just who a given people are, how they can be counted on to behave, even whether one can rely on them in business or political and social life. The case law enables justice to function in society; the Ten Commandments kind of law makes life in community possible. A good analogy is to think of the Ten Commandments kind of law as akin to the Preamble to the U.S. Constitution and its Bill of Rights, while the case law is akin to the statutes and precedents of the U.S. code and the laws of the individual states.

Scholars have pointed out that Israel's law collections, in particular the whole book of Deuteronomy, resemble ancient Middle Eastern treaties between a ruler and the groups of peoples or lands on which he rules. The form of such treaties is not identical with the book of Deuteronomy and other biblical law collections, but it is similar. Treaties often open with a preamble that describes what the ruler has done for his subject peoples, sets out the terms of their new relationship, warns (often with a list of curses) them of the consequences of disobedience, and sketches the blessings that will follow from compliance. Such treaties often end with a list of those who have signed as witnesses to the treaty. Such lists may include the names of the deities worshiped by the monarch and his people.

Clearly, the Ten Commandments are not a complete treaty in the form just described. Surrounding the Ten Commandments in the book of Exodus there are elements of such a treaty form (see Exod. 23:20–33, which closes the law collection that begins in chap. 21, and also Exod. 24:3–8, which tells of the covenant ceremony itself), but these are not a direct part of the "Ten Words" (see Exod. 34:28; Deut. 4:13; 10:4). Even so, the Ten Commandments are a kind of treaty between God and the people. The more familiar language is covenant, a compact between two parties that both agree to hold sacred. Earlier covenants spell out the meaning. God's covenant with Noah and his descendants (that is, all humankind) and with the earth and all its creatures assures that never again will God bring a great flood. The conditions for life on earth are guaranteed by God. No demand is made on the earth or its creatures beyond those already found in the story of creation (see Gen. 8 and 9).

God also made a covenant with Abraham and his descendants, once again taking on full responsibility for fulfilling the words of promise made to Abraham when he was summoned to leave Haran for the land of Canaan (see Gen. 12:1–3; chap. 15; 35:9–15). This covenant, too, offers no specific demands. It assures the ancestors of Israel that God has selected them and their descendants for a very specific vocation in the world, assuring them that God will also provide a land, blessing, and many descendants as they fulfill that mission.

With the giving of the Ten Commandments a new element enters the picture. God now calls for fidelity to Torah, God's teaching or guiding principles. Now, on the sacred mountain, God is providing a gift that means their very life, as the book of Deuteronomy says (see Deut. 30). God extends a gift of love, but the gift does bring demands. Israel is called to "obey my voice and keep my covenant" (Exod. 19:5). Of course, Abraham and his sons and grandsons were also expected to follow in the path God laid out for them, but the demands of the covenant were implicit, not stated. Here they are set forth, and the Ten Commandments are the groundwork for all of God's demands to the human community, entrusted to Israel.

Dos and Don'ts

Basically, the Ten Commandments tell us what not to do. Even the two that are stated positively, Sabbath observance and honoring of parents, can easily be put in negative form like the others—and perhaps they were originally negative in form too: "Do not do any work on the seventh day" and " Do not dishonor your father and mother." Is this negative form troubling? Other commands of the Old and New Testaments are put positively: "You shall love the LORD your God with all your heart" (Deut. 6:5) and "You shall love your neighbor as yourself" (Lev. 19:18). Jesus states these commandments positively too, and the Sermon on the Mount (Matt. 5–7) is largely positive.

We mustn't overlook the value of the negatively stated commandment, however. When we are speaking about human conduct and are seeking to affirm its very foundation, the negatively put statement is immensely useful, just because it is negative. As we have noted above, these short prohibitions rule out certain forms of conduct. At the same time, they invite, even require, the community and its individual members to ponder and work at the question of just what exactly is being prohibited. What does it mean, precisely, to "have no other God [or gods] before [or besides] the LORD"? The community must work that out. The negative form actually helps, for it does not give a specific definition; rather, it describes an activity that must be avoided. Similarly, the command "You shall not kill" opens up a huge set of questions. Clearly, one may kill animals for food, according to the biblical texts (at least after the flood of Noah's day), so the reference is to human beings. But the Bible calls for capital punishment under certain circumstances, and it assumes killing in warfare. Each of the commandments in turn opens up issues and questions that the community must address. And that means that every community, in its own time and circumstances, will have to look at these commandments for itself. What the commandments do is affirm that a wholesome life in communion with God and with one's fellow human beings is endangered if these prohibitions are violated.

Many questions remain and simply have to be addressed—and therein lies the strength of the negative form of the commandments. That negative form calls the community to discussion, debate, and action. The negative form, however, gives guidance to the debate. "Whatever else you do, Israelites (or Americans), do not work seven days a week. Stop and rest. Find time for reflection and for renewal of life." "Whatever else you do, Israelites (and Americans), do not treat life lightly. Honor life, cherish it, nurture it, preserve it. But do so in light of all of life's conditions, responsibilities, and opportunities."

Sometimes, a society just does not know what the best thing to do actually is. But we can more easily see when a given course of action is wrong, or even unbearable. Think of the atrocities of our recent years! The world community may not have known, or known soon enough, what to do about the civil war that befell the lands of former Yugoslavia, but that community knew for certain that the conflict simply had to end. Similarly, in Rwanda, atrocities against one tribe by another tribe continued entirely too long before the world community found its voice of outraged protest. That voice is still not strong enough about events in southern Sudan.

The prophet Amos once spoke about Israel's self-indulgent disregard of the plight of others with the phrase "but [they] are not grieved over the ruin of Joseph" (Amos 6:6). Our basic commandments give us ground for cries of protest and outrage, even when we may not know exactly what we ought positively to recommend. The parable in the Gospel of Luke makes this point (Luke 18:1–8): The unjust judge may not care a fig about justice, but when the widow persists in her demand that the judge do his duty, she gets results at last, since she simply could not endure to forgo justice. She could not give herself justice; that was the job of the judge. The widow's indispensable duty was to cry out against injustice. Many protest movements throughout history have learned that lesson. It does not always work, for some structures seem impervious to protest and calls for fairness and justice. But sometimes it works, to the good of all involved.

Avoiding Legalism

We know that, even though love is the setting and presupposition of law and commandment, a legalistic attitude is surely possible. Communities and individuals through the centuries have suffered from legalism—an application of the gift of law that makes law into an instrument of control of others and coercive pressure to make others conform to our understanding of law. How can legalism be avoided? Some people seem to know with great precision how the rest of us should behave, and they are all too ready to appeal to biblical laws in support of their views. Once again, the very brevity, and the negative form of the Ten Commandments, helps avoid legalism. When my grandfather sought to control all the activities of his grandchildren on the Sabbath, my parents would simply say, "What is forbidden is work, not play." When today some appeal to a few texts that denounce certain forms of sexual behavior, others have a right to point out that the Ten Commandments say nothing about anything other than adultery; Jesus says nothing about homosexuality.

The Commandments as a Holy Gift

Two places in the biblical world stand out as the most holy sites known to the Jewish and Christian communities: Mount Sinai and Jerusalem. Neither is holy in and of itself; they are made holy by encounters with God and by God's special disclosures. God's law, sealed in covenant, is revealed at Mount Sinai. God's meeting with the community at the site of the temple in Jerusalem and (for Christians) on a hill just outside the city have made Jerusalem a place of holiness for countless Jews and Christians.

The texts surrounding the Ten Commandments reveal this holiness, the awesome character of Mount Sinai. As the revelation is about to take place, the people are warned repeatedly to keep their distance (Exod. 19). Once the covenant ceremony is enacted (Exod. 24:3–8),

Moses and other leaders ascend the mountain, have a sacred meal, and see the underside of God's throne-chariot, gleaming like sapphire. Moses goes farther up the mountain and there receives the commandments, in particular the Ten Commandments, written by God on stone tablets, we are told (Exod. 24:9–14). And as the revelation is taking place, cloud and storm and flashes of lightning turn the mountaintop into a "devouring fire" (24:17).

During the next forty days, the community came to believe that Moses must have perished in that consuming fire. Chapters 32–34 complete the scene, with two settings, one in the valley, where Aaron is persuaded by the people to make a golden calf as the emblem of God and to proceed on their journey without Moses. The other scene, atop the mountain, reveals Moses pleading with God for the life of the people. Just as God reveals the Ten Commandments on the holy mountain, the people violate its first two prohibitions in the valley below.

Violence follows when Moses confronts Aaron and the worshipers of the calf. Again Moses pleads with God in behalf of the people (Exod. 32). Next, Moses ascends the mountain, seeking an even more intimate encounter with God (Exod. 33). Moses, placed by God in a cleft of the rocky mountainside, covered by God's hand, is permitted to hear God pronounce the divine name and to see the backside of God. The scene powerfully reveals both the intimacy of Moses' relation with God and the mystery that always accompanies God's acts of revelation. Moses had broken the first tablets of the Ten Commandments (chap. 32); now he receives a second set. As he comes down the mountain, his long and intimate association with God causes his face to glow with the shared glory of the Deity. Moses must wear a mask, for a while, to shield the people from this shared glory of God. Small wonder that the Ten Commandments, along with all of the law revealed at Mount Sinai, is so foundational for Israel. Law (torah in Hebrew) partakes of the very presence and glory of God.

Keeping the Commandments

As noted above, Moses pled earnestly with God not to destroy the faithless Israelites who had made a golden calf at the very time that God was providing the torah. Actually, Moses offers two prayers in

Exodus 32. In the first one (32:11–13), Moses reminds the Deity that the Egyptians might get the wrong picture of God if God should destroy the freed slaves, concluding that God was evil and malicious, never intending to make a new life for Moses and his people. Moses also made the point that God had already promised the ancestors that they would be blessed with land and descendants and the continuing care of God's presence. God had a stake in the future of Israel!

The second prayer, which comes after the people have been severely punished, is even more powerful (32:30–32). Moses acknowledges that the people have "sinned a great sin." They have violated the first two of the Ten Commandments, setting up an idol and worshiping it as God. Moses pleads with God to forgive them—freely to forgive them, for Moses makes no promises or vows in return. And if not, then Moses makes the remarkable request: "Blot me out of [your] book"! If the people must die, then Moses wishes to die. Perhaps Moses is even saying, "Take my life instead!" In any event, these two prayers of Moses in Exodus 32 are a powerful reminder that the Ten Commandments are destined to be broken. When they are broken, then, like Moses, violators are called on to turn to God for forgiveness.

The fact that individuals and groups violate the Ten Commandments does not make them less valuable. Violators do indeed offend God and harm individuals and the community. But, as Paul tells the Romans, "If it had not been for the law, I would not have known sin" (Rom. 7:7). The law makes explicit what one by nature (see Rom. 1:19–20) should already sense. Violations of the law are serious and destructive, but the law is still there to assist one not to violate the law again. It is difficult to know just how much of a deterrence the Ten Commandments may be in a given society, but it is certain that acts of repentance and acts to repair the damage done strengthen individuals and the community to be more faithful to the commandments next time.

The Commandments and the New Testament

We should never overlook the severity of Jesus' commands in the Sermon on the Mount (Matt. 5–7). The message of this opening part of the Christian "good news" describes how life is to be lived, here on earth, in God's renewed and transformed community. Even now, the gospel message claims, that "kingdom of heaven," as it is called, is being created here on earth, as a small band of Jesus' followers claim the power of God's Spirit to live faithful and peaceable and responsible lives. They are to be "perfect" (Matt. 5:48), just as God in heaven is perfect. Israel's prophets had portrayed this coming day on which peace with justice would prevail worldwide. Jesus tells his hearers that they need wait no longer for that day. All the resources required for a just and faithful and peaceable life are at hand: now claim those resources and live as you were intended and destined to live! What more does God need to do? What resources are missing? Is the way not clear?

The commandments of the new covenant mesh with those of the earlier covenants. Jesus intensifies the demands, just as he underlines the cosmic love of God for all the world, saint and sinner alike, a love that, as we have seen, transforms demand into gift and shows how gift leads to demand. Jesus clearly has special concern for the poor and the oppressed and the unloved, and he also has special concern for those who have violated the commandments. "Go your way, and . . . do not sin again," he tells one notorious sinner (John 8:11). Law and love go together, not just because God's love precedes God's demands. Rather, God's demands and our faithfulness to God's demands are—both of them—*expressions of love*: God's love for us and our love for God and our neighbors.

Questions for Discussion

1. What difference does it make when one understands the commandments as an expression of divine love? What does that suggest about the nature and purpose of God's demands on our lives?
2. What is the difference between case law and categorical law? Why are both important to a community?
3. How can we honor the Ten Commandments and avoid slipping into a legalistic attitude?

2

God Is One

You shall have no other gods before me.
You shall not make for yourself an idol. . . .
You shall not make wrongful use of the name of the LORD your God.
— Exodus 20:3, 4, 7

*T*he first three commandments belong together. They all have to do with God's exclusive claim on the human community—as ancient Israel understood that claim.[1]

As we noted in the first chapter, the commandments themselves developed from originally brief, pithy, negative statements summarizing those forms of human behavior that were simply not tolerable. Additions were made to some of them to clarify just what the basic statement meant. The meaning of these first three commandments clearly developed over time, as the clarifying additions to the second commandment indicate.

The first commandment probably underwent three changes in basic meaning, even though the stages no doubt overlapped in time. Originally the commandment prohibited the worship of any deity except YHWH, Israel's God who brought the slaves from Egypt and made covenant with them at Mount Sinai. Other gods there were, of course, but Israel was not to worship them. The second commandment, building on the first, forbade the placing of images of other gods at the places where Israel's God YHWH was worshiped. Note the references to the burial or putting away of foreign gods at Israelite sanctuaries in Genesis 35:2–4 and Joshua 24:23–25.

The second stage is reflected in the story of Elijah's contest with the Canaanite deity Baal, reported in 1 Kings 18. Here, the situation has changed. YHWH and Baal are rival deities, and the community is charged by Elijah to stop "limping with two different opinions" (1 Kgs. 18:21). Elijah calls for exclusive worship of YHWH, as before, but he denies that Baal has the power that his worshipers attribute to him. YHWH alone has that power and alone deserves to be called God. Rival claimants to deity are put to the test on Mount Carmel. YHWH is the winner, and the priests of Baal are slaughtered by Elijah. "My god is better than your god" becomes the slogan, and the fruit of such intolerance shows up in the time of King Jehu (2 Kgs. 9–11).

This second stage often seems to follow directly from the first. A great revelation of the nature and character of a deity takes place, and a new religious understanding is born. This new understanding claims its followers deeply and produces passionate commitment, as in Moses' day. God is to be worshiped in a given way, and that way rules out other ways. But in the second stage something is added: other ways of understanding—and those who hold to those ways—are not to be tolerated. This exclusive devotion is admirable but troubling. It is at this point that the wedding of religion and politics often occurs, bringing bigotry and intolerance. For Elijah, apparently, the worshipers of Baal were to be humiliated and discredited, and their leaders destroyed. Religious conflicts around the globe today echo Elijah's understanding.

The third stage is that of Israel's prophets, where the revolutionary import of the first commandment shows up clearly. This third stage first insists, as with Amos (see Amos 1–2), that Israel's God YHWH is also the sovereign Lord of the nations of earth, not just Israel's God. This understanding is underscored and magnificently presented in the poetry of Isaiah 40–55. There is one God of the universe. All nations and peoples are subjects of this one God. Israel knows God's name as YHWH, but YHWH is the Incomparable One, mysterious, merciful and compassionate, but also powerful, even irresistible.

This understanding of God as One has a splendid statement in Deuteronomy 6:4–5: "Hear, O Israel: The LORD is our God, the LORD alone." This text affirms the first meaning of the first commandment: YHWH alone is to be worshiped as God. It does not call for the extermination of other deities (though, of course, other language in Deuteronomy and elsewhere unhappily does do so), but calls for loving devotion to YHWH with all one's powers (Deut. 6:5). But this text also affirms the third stage, for it makes clear that Israel's God is God alone, is the one God of the universe.

But what of pluralism? Is not this very notion of the oneness of God bound to lead to intolerance and bigotry? It need not and must not. This understanding of the oneness of God has many immensely valuable features, some of which will be noted below. But first let's consider how the oneness of God might not only allow for religious diversity and pluralism but applaud and affirm it. Might we not simply declare that this Israelite understanding is right? The very definition of God, one may claim, implies unity. There can be only one reality deserving of the name God. If one worships God under any name, one worships the one God, for there is but one God. There are many ways of perceiving God, of experiencing God, of naming God, of worshiping God, but all that variety, by all its names and in all its nuances, is finally directed to the one God.

How different that understanding is from the first understanding! For many societies throughout the history of the planet, human beings have experienced a plurality of powers and numinous presences that were understood to be transcendent powers, powers of the world beyond the world of ordinary human experience. Often, these powers were understood to be not a happy family of deities, but rival powers, requiring worshipers to respond in a variety of ways. How could worshipers please one deity without offending another? Elaborate rituals developed to secure blessing and avoid harm from the transcendent powers.

The prophets' notion of the oneness of God places all that anxiety in one basket: Israel and all peoples have to deal with one God and one God alone. This understanding is pinned down for the Israelite community in the opening chapters of the Bible: Genesis 1 and 2. God the Creator calls into being every thing, every creature, every person in the universe. There are two kinds of reality: there is God, and there are realities created by God. What a revolution in human thought that is!

Of course, such an understanding brings its difficulties. When there is a plurality of deities, then evil can be explained as having its origin in some conflict among the gods. In strict monotheism, how can evil be adequately accounted for? And this applies to so-called natural evils (earthquake, volcano, plague, famine) as well as to moral evil. One can make better sense of actual human experience with a plurality of gods.

But consider the other human experiences and longings that a monotheistic faith provides. When there is one, and only one, transcendent reality with which (whom) to deal, worshipers are required to assign responsibility for both good and evil to themselves or to God, or to the mysterious outworkings of a good creation. Anxiety does not disappear, but it is focused. God is involved in good and God is involved in evil (see Isa. 45:7). Human beings too are involved in both. Life is relational; there is God, and there are the persons and things that God has called into being, both intimately involved in the ongoing processes of life in God's good universe.

One other positive feature of the unity of God should be mentioned. There seems to be some special appeal within the human psyche for partnership, for union, with one beloved being. Just as the commandments arise in the context of divine love (chap. 1 above), so also the first commandment stresses the unity of God because Israel is drawn to God by the power of praise, thanksgiving, and love. The confessional statement in Exodus 19:4 states this relationship very well, from God's side: "You have seen what I did to the Egyptians, and how I bore you on eagles' wings and brought you to *myself*" (italics added). Israel comes not only to a holy mountain but to YHWH, drawn by love. And the other confessional statement mentioned above, Deuteronomy 6:5, calls for love for God in return. The analogy with human love is surely appropriate: God and human beings are bound to one another in love as are husband and wife, and human beings are the better able to love in return when they recognize the unity, the oneness, of God. God is One, and human beings, created in God's image and likeness (Gen. 1:26), are also God's special partner in love, for the good of the creation.

To affirm God's oneness and God's companionship in love, however, left much of the mystery of God's being and purpose for the universe hidden, unstated. The very name of God disclosed to Moses at the sacred mountain (Exod. 3) is at once hidden and revealed: "I AM WHO I AM" (Exod. 3:14) most probably represents a refusal to give to Moses some inner meaning of the name YHWH on the basis of which he would have special powers, as we will see when we discuss the third commandment below. This meaning is borne out by the enigmatic statement of God's name in Exodus 33, where Moses is permitted to see only God's back and is given the assertion, "I will be gracious to whom I will be gracious, and will show mercy on whom I will show mercy" (Exod. 33:19).

The mystery of God's inner being serves an enormously important purpose. It helps to protect the community from claiming too much about the meaning of God's revelation. The first commandment affirms the unity of God, but it does not follow that all peoples and individuals must understand God's oneness *in just the way that ancient Israel understood that oneness.* Israel never abandoned this profound understanding of God's hiddenness, and the church too knows that God is both hidden and revealed. See 1 John 4:12: "No one has ever seen God; if we love one another, God lives in us, and his love is perfected in us."

"You Shall Not Make for Yourself an Idol"

The second commandment follows directly from the first. To make a three-dimensional representation of one's God was the almost universal practice of ancient peoples. Surely the Israelites knew that representations of a deity in wood or clay or metal images were intended to bring the presence and power of the deity close to them in daily life. The worshiper knew the difference between the deity who transcended daily life and this way of representing the deity through an image. But for Israel, such images were idols. The Hebrew term *pesel* meant a carved, shaped, or poured three-dimensional representation of God.

God was, of course, represented in the life of the Israelite community in a number of ways. God came in dreams, in stories, and even in particular places, and was invisibly present in sacred objects such as the Ark and the Tent. God was known to be present in the Jerusalem temple, but even there the descriptions of God's presence made it clear that God's freedom to appear or not to appear was never compromised. Israel had no control over God or God's power apart from the persuasive power of prayer and faithful conduct.

Why was the community so adamant about the making of images? No fully adequate explanation has been given, I believe, but there are pointers. In the first place, the distinction made above in the discussion of the first commandment between God the Creator and all else as a creation of God is one pointer. How can any created reality, no matter how sublime, do justice to God's transcendent character, God's mystery, God's beauty and glory? But one might object that the makers of images can well appreciate the limitation of their representation of God while still finding it useful and an important aid in giving God due praise.

Another pointer is that the intimacy of association with the image on the part of the worshiper can lead to a false notion that the worshiper has control of the deity and can manipulate the power of God for the worshiper's own ends. Both of these pointers are important, as we can see from later biblical history. Prophets can speak out against the most holy objects of Israel if those objects become instruments through which Israel seeks to coerce God's blessing. Jeremiah spoke of those who chanted the refrain "The temple of the LORD, the temple of the LORD, the temple of the LORD" (Jer. 7:4). Not even the holy temple was permitted to serve as a guarantee of God's presence and protection. Should God see fit, Zion would be plowed as a field (Mic. 3:12). The second commandment is about God's freedom from all coercion. God gladly accepted gifts from the community, but multiplying the gifts assured nothing, no matter how costly the gifts. See the remarkable summary in Micah 6:1–8.

Surely, however, worshipers knew the difference between seeking to coerce God to act and praying and pleading for God to do so. The prayers of the Bible are full of pleas, even desperate pleas, for God to act. See Isaiah 63:7–64:12; Psalm 44; and the almost truculent tone of a prayer of Moses in Exodus 32:11–14 and its parallel in Deuteronomy 9:25–29. Some of these prayers involve acknowledgment of Israel's failures, but occasionally, as in Psalm 44, the community insists that there is no correlation whatever between the community's failings and the calamities that have befallen them. The whole book of Job has this discontinuity as its theme. In short, it is clearly in order to plead with God for help and blessing. It is even in order to call God to account, as Abraham did: "Shall not the Judge of all the earth do what is just?" (Gen. 18:25). Such prayers are not coercive; they reveal the extent to which Israel saw itself in partnership with YHWH.

One other possible pointer to the meaning of the commandment may be of help. Genesis 1:26 asserts that God created human beings in the divine image and likeness. The terms "image" (Hebrew *tselem*) and "likeness" (Hebrew *demuth*) certainly point to an intimacy of association between God and human beings that was understood to be unique to the human community. It must also have involved some kind of understanding of how human beings—to some limited extent—were to represent God and God's causes and purposes in the world. See the extraordinary language of Psalm 8! Might it be, then, that for Israel to have made images of God was forbidden because the only appropriate representation of deity in the creation was: frail and imperfect humankind! To lavish undue attention on three-dimensional representations of God might distract human beings from their created task of representing God's cause in the world—through the threefold task laid on the human community as stated by the prophet Micah: "to do justice, and to love kindness, and to walk humbly with your God" (Mic. 6:8).

Sometimes we overlook, I fear, the positive import of these first two commandments for the human community and for worshiping communities in particular. We noted above how important it is for a community to recognize the oneness of God and thereby avoid being trapped into trying to placate a host of rival deities. For the ancient Greek world, the all too human features of their gods led to widespread rejection of the whole religious system. The same has happened in many lands today, when the sheer proliferation of religious beliefs and practices has discredited all such belief and practice.

Monotheism does not remove the possibility of being overwhelmed by fear and dread of God, of course, but it does focus the fear. And coupled with the understanding that God's reality cannot be fully known by human beings, remaining always transcendent of our images and symbols, our theologies, and our practices of worship and devotion, one can step back from traditional dogma and custom, remind oneself that our religious understandings and traditions *approximate* the truth and glory of God's true character but do not do God justice. The first two commandments seek to rule out excessive claims for our knowledge of God's ways, God's character, God's very being.

The second commandment did not rule out artistic expression of the community's religious experience and understandings. It focused their expressions. The Bible itself is Israel's major artistic gift to the world. Its narratives, its wisdom, its poetry, its visions of a world made righteous and faithful and beautiful—all these demonstrate that the prohibition of image making did not eliminate the pursuit of artistic visions. Jewish, Christian, and Muslim artists have not been intimidated by the prohibition against representing the deity in sculpture. One might even claim that, in this instance as in so many others, the prohibition of a particular kind of human activity only presses the community to understand better what in fact is prohibited and why, and to claim with enthusiasm the remaining vast arena of freedom that the prohibition has helped to open up.

"You Shall Not Make Wrongful Use of the Name of the LORD Your God"

The familiar translation of the third commandment is, "Do not take the name of the LORD your God in vain." The Hebrew term translated "in vain" does sometimes mean vanity or emptiness, but it also means moral worthlessness or even evildoing. The command prohibits misuse of God's name.

What is a misuse of God's name? Much more is intended than cursing and foul speech. The third commandment has a broader purpose. It rules out any uses of God's name to do harm to *anyone*. Praying for God to curse one's enemies is bad enough, but preying on the religious beliefs and anxieties of others for one's own gain or purposes is far worse. This commandment is of special importance for religious leaders, for the temptation to use the power of religious belief for personal gain has always been hard for some to resist.

Using God's name to do harm can be as base and corrupt as simply perverting the religious system for personal profit or self-indulgence, which was the case with the sons of Eli (1 Sam. 2:12–17) and also with Samuel's sons (1 Sam. 8:1–3). More dangerous by far is the temptation Hosea identified among Israel's priests. He claimed that they "feed on the sin of [the] people" and are "greedy for their iniquity" (Hos. 4:8). That is, the very failings of the people were welcomed by the religious leaders, for the more the people sinned, the richer the priests became. If only such temptation had been confined to the days of Hosea!

This commandment flatly asserts that no one is to use the power of religion to gain personal or political advantage over others. Obviously, the commandment affects the lives and conduct of professional religious leaders in direct and inescapable ways. Religious leaders have the weighty task of interpreting their religious community's revelations and traditions faithfully while also seeking further guidance from God. Israel's prophets recognized the ease with which religious leaders could accept the desires of the king as God's desires, giving the king just what he wanted to hear—all in the name of God. See 1 Kings 22 for a detailed picture of faithful and unfaithful prophets.

There were no completely reliable tests of the truth of a prophetic revelation in ancient Israel, and (so far as I can see) there are no completely reliable tests today. Israel's prophets did struggle with the issue, and they left good guidelines, including the following. These guidelines are implied in the story from 1 Kings 22, mentioned above. The kings of Israel and Judah gathered at the city of Samaria to decide whether or not to go to war against Syria (Aram). Four hundred prophets called for war. Jehoshaphat, the king of Judah, asked for a second opinion, thereby offering one criterion of true prophecy. If prophets agree too readily with what the ruler desires to do, beware! Even so, we know that sometimes prophets simply like to object, to show their opposition, and stubbornly resist anything proposed by the authorities.

In our story, the lone dissenter, Micaiah, offered a second implied criterion. He said that God was not in support of the war, but the king could go out and see. If he returned victorious, then Micaiah would be repudiated. Such a criterion is of little value in policy making. It only enables one side or the other to say, "I told you so."

A third implied criterion is also present in this story. Micaiah describes a vision of God seated on a throne with the angelic host gathered around. A discussion ensues, followed by the decision that one of the assembly's messengers will go down and deceive the four hundred prophets. The implied criterion, I suggest, is that a true prophet is one who can offer convincing, credible evidence that he or she is trustworthy. Has the prophet "stood in [God's] council," as the prophet Jeremiah put it (Jer 23:22)? But Jeremiah (23:28) warns against the mere telling of dreams or visions, demanding that prophets speak God's word truthfully, faithfully, reliably (all three adverbs apply to the Hebrew term *'emeth*).

One other direct criterion of true or false prophecy appears in Deuteronomy 13: any prophet who calls for the worship of other gods is to be rejected, even if the prophet does signs and wonders and clearly appears to have wonder-working powers. The presence of miracle-working powers is not sufficient proof of the authenticity of a prophetic word. The core tradition of the community is itself an immensely valuable criterion, when wisely used.

We can see that none of these criteria of the true prophet is absolutely fail-proof. They do help, however, in offering guidance for religious leaders today who wish to honor the third commandment. Making "wrongful use of the name of the LORD your God" would surely include a host of religious practices that are present, it seems, in all the major religions today. The worst of these is to convince fellow believers that God desires or requires that they blow themselves to pieces in order to take the lives of as many individuals as possible from the enemy camp. Who can deny that such action is making wrongful use of the name of God?

Wrongful use can be much more subtle. The criterion for true prophecy found in Deuteronomy 13 rightly supports the view that a religious community has its core beliefs that are surely to be upheld at all cost. The issue is how such core beliefs are to be presented. Does the mystery of God, who claims us totally, remain, or has that mystery been laid out in such detail that dogmatism or fundamentalism is the result? Is it permissible to threaten nonbelievers with hellfire, or should the community leave with a merciful but just God the fate of unbelievers? Do the core beliefs become so specific and detailed as to force the religious community into monitoring the social, economic, and cultural practices of a total, pluralistic community?

The first three commandments offer immensely valuable guidance, I believe, for all religious communities today. In a fragmented and bewilderingly diverse religious world, the assertion that there is one, only one, transcendent reality to whom (which) the entire universe owes its existence and its direction does not deny at all that there is a rich and humanly enriching variety of ways of understanding and affirming the reality of this one God. God's demands on the human community as stated in these first three commandments all clearly aim at the welfare of the entire universe. God demands only what makes for life and blessing. It is liberating to confront only one ultimate reality, liberating to be reminded of the enormous trust placed in the human community to care for the world and honor its creatures and its inanimate elements, all of which are God's creation. It is liberating to be required to let God's powers work for the good of all and not to seek to divert them to our own personal or ideological ends.

The following commandments build on these first three, addressing in a variety of ways what it means to be created in the divine image and likeness and required to share the divine purposes and to seek out the ways of God for the good of the whole creation.

Questions for Discussion

1. What are the practical implications of affirming the oneness of God?
2. How does the prohibition against the making of idols help us understand the relationship between God and human beings?
3. How are we tempted to misuse God's name today?

3

Sabbath and Family

Remember the sabbath day, and keep it holy.
Honor your father and your mother.

—Exodus 20:8, 12

*T*he next two commandments also belong together. They provide a bridge between the first three commandments and the last five. And what an important bridge this is! The Sabbath is a gift of God for the sake of the human community, but it is also a gift *to* God. God rests on the Sabbath, taking delight in the workings of the creation (Gen. 2:2–3). Sabbath observance forms a bridge between earth and heaven, strengthening the ties that bind the human community to God and fellow human beings to one another.

The same is true for the family. From the very beginning of human life, according to the Bible, family was a necessity. Not until both male and female are created is life in the garden complete (Gen. 2). And God forms a part of that completeness, coming in the cool of the evening to spend time and share life with the first human pair. Indeed, when Cain is condemned to isolation from family and community, he finds his life unbearable, and God acts to make life at least tolerable for the first person to turn in rage on a family member (Gen. 4).

Both Sabbath and family enable the human community to share and to deepen its companionship with God. At the same time, both Sabbath and family help fit the human community for responsible personal and social existence in God's world. And both institutions are in grave peril today.

Origins of the Sabbath

The origin of the observance of one day in seven as a day of rest is unknown. Many explanations have been offered, but none of them is satisfactory, in my judgment. At some time early in Israel's history, the Sabbath emerges as a day of rest from labor. It is possible that its beginnings lay with celebrations connected with the phases of the moon, since new moon and Sabbath observances are mentioned together occasionally (Amos 8:5; Isa. 1:13). Perhaps the Sabbath originally marked the full moon, paralleling the observance of the new moon. If so, we have no satisfactory explanation for its becoming a seventh-day observance, ignoring the phases of the moon.

Other explanations have been offered. In Mesopotamia, days of ill omen were known, sometimes in multiples of seven. Those days were considered unsuitable for various kinds of undertakings, but it seems unlikely that dark days like these could have given rise to the Sabbath as known in Israel—a day of rest and rejoicing in YHWH.

Seven-day-long fasts and festivals are known in some ancient Near Eastern societies. Did the Sabbath develop from such seven-day events, closing them with a day of rest? If so, we have no trace of a biblical connection between Sabbath and other festivals, other than the connection with the new moon mentioned above. Market days also have been suggested; perhaps seven-day-long market gatherings ending with a day of festivities contributed to the Sabbath's origin. Market days, however, are not known to follow a seven-day pattern.

Some have suggested, finally, that Kenite metalsmiths (Gen. 4:22) seem to have had connections with early Israelite life and with the worship of YHWH (Exod. 18 and Judg. 1:16 tell of Moses' connection with the Midianites/Kenites). Metalsmiths need to cool their fires for rest periodically. Might their rest day have contributed to the origin of the Sabbath? Such a connection would place the beginning of the Sabbath in close connection with Moses and the wilderness wanderings. Moreover, this explanation would fit the character of the Sabbath as a rest day. But the theory is no more than speculation; we have no direct evidence in support of it.

We are left, then, with two of the prohibitions of the Ten Commandments—the prohibition of idol making and the observance of the

Sabbath—that stand out as entirely distinct commands, not easily accounted for by cultural realities common to Israel and its neighbors. The first of these, idol making, however, easily arises out of the first commandment as an extension and elaboration of it. Not so the Sabbath; it has no clear antecedents in Israel or in the lives of Israel's neighbors. It can be called a unique Israelite institution.

The Meaning of the Sabbath

What are people to do on the Sabbath? We are told in detail what Israel is to do on its festal days—on Passover, Pentecost/Weeks, and Tabernacles (see Lev. 23 and Num. 28–29 for the fullest description). Not so with the Sabbath. It is to be a rest day, that is clear, and for both human beings (Israelite and non-Israelite, slave and free) and farm animals (see Exod. 23:12 as well as Exod. 20:8–11 and Deut. 5:12–15). In fact, the Sabbath is hallowed, kept holy, not by any religious observances or duties at all. It is hallowed by *rest*, by stopping the normal activities of workdays and ceasing work (the Hebrew verb *shbt* means "to stop, to cease"). A proper observance of the Sabbath is leaving aside the bodily and intellectual and artistic labors that support one throughout six days in order to be refreshed from such labors. Just as the day is divided into daytime for labor and night for rest, so the week also is divided into six days for labor and one for rest. For all the Israelites, all work was to cease: no shearing of sheep, no tending of the grapevines, no gathering of olives, no planting or harvesting of barley or wheat. No repairing of the house or fence or plowing of the field. All normal activities were to cease, for the day of rest had dawned.

Exodus 20:11 ties the Sabbath directly to God's rest following the creation of the universe. Genesis 2:2–3 says that God observed the Sabbath, the first Sabbath ever, rested from divine labors, and hallowed it. How did God hallow, or sanctify ("make holy," "set apart for a special use") the Sabbath? Simply by resting. That was the best possible, the most convincing, example that could have been provided. If God rested on the Sabbath day, how could the community not rest?

In later times, of course, the community would need to decide just what kinds of human activity qualified as work. When the seventh day dawned, some human activities still had to be carried on: care for the sick, interventions in times of emergency, and the covering of those activities that simply could not wait for a full day. But, basically, when the seventh day dawned normal activities ceased. Even if it was harvesttime and rain threatened, one waited until the next day to harvest the barley or the wheat. Even if the olives or the figs were ripe and ready to be gathered, they had to wait for one more day. It was Sabbath day.

Like all the other commandments, the Sabbath commandment was intended for the enrichment and enhancement of life. Even if it was originally put in negative form, say, "You shall not dishonor the Sabbath day," the intention was positive and affirmative of life. Sabbath observance meant rest from labor—at a time when there were no unions to bargain with management and no governmental laws or guidelines to provide relief for workers. It assured all members of the society, the rich and the poor, the citizen and the stranger, the free citizen and the slave, and even the farm animals, that one day in seven was a time of rest and refreshment of life. If even God rests, then surely the remainder of the creation can be permitted to rest.

How Sabbath Was Observed

In ancient Israel, no doubt, there were workaholics just as there are today. Some persons may take to rest as ducks take to water; for them, rest is the easiest thing in the world. For others, however, rest doesn't come naturally. There is always more to be done. When the weekend comes, one has opportunity to catch up on tasks not adequately seen to during the week. Some persons regularly count on the so-called rest day to complete work not done during the five- or six-day week. And some persons are simply miserable if not working.

We do not know, of course, just what ancient Israelites did with their Sabbath days, but we can well surmise what they must have done. Think of the enormous gift that a seventh day of rest must have been for Israel! Is it too much to suppose that we would not have had our sacred Scriptures, humanly speaking, if there had been no Sabbath? The seventh day of rest meant *time*—time for the parents' education of their children, time for telling the stories of God's dealings with Israel, time for prophets to prepare their words of judgment and promise, time for psalmists to shape and test their praises and prayers, time for the wise teachers to instruct their young pupils, and time to commune with the Lord of the Sabbath. The community had time to deal with life's enigmas: how could God allow evildoers to prosper while the faithful struggled to keep body and soul together? How could God permit cruel nations to oppress the people chosen as the apple of God's eye? How could God let plagues and famines and earthquakes and tornados work their dreadful destruction on communities that had done nothing—or, at least, little—to warrant such catastrophes?

It seems certain that the great literary heritage of Israel found in what we Christians call the Old Testament owes its very existence to the fact that Israel had *time*—holy time—in which to think and study and brood and seek God's inspiration and guidance. During the Babylonian exile (587–538 BCE) the community apparently was able to observe its Sabbath, at least to some extent (see, for example, Ezek. 11:16; 22:8), for it was during this time that much of the Hebrew Scriptures took its present shape. It is hard to overestimate the importance of Israel's Sabbath; its very life seems to have been tied to this divine gift, this blessed command.

Sabbath Joy

In my childhood, Sabbath observance was strictly enforced by my grandfather, but there was little joy in it. Like all good gifts of a good God, Sabbath too could be spoiled by those who, ironically, deeply treasured it. In Jesus' day too such Sabbath observers apparently existed. A day of rejoicing in the gifts of God could of course be transmuted into a day of punctilious religiosity. Jesus' warning, "The sabbath was made for humankind, and not humankind for the sabbath" (Mark 2:27), condemns such understandings.

But the Sabbath was not normally that kind of day for the Jewish community. It was a joy and a delight. In particular, the study of God's dealings with Israel, the Torah (our Old Testament), was like honey on the lips (Psalm 19). Psalmists could exclaim, "Oh, how I love your law!" (Ps. 119:97). This savoring of the story of God's deeds of deliverance of Israel over the centuries, amplified by words of prophets and sages and poets who sought to understand God's deeds, must surely have taken place on the Sabbath, when there was time to address the glories and the misery of human life. The community knew also that God, the sovereign creator of the universe, was also studying Torah and resting on the seventh day.

The Sabbath and the Lord's Day

During the first Christian century, the early Christian community continued to observe the Sabbath. To it, they added gatherings on the first day of the week, Sunday, for the celebration of the day of Jesus' resurrection. And so the Christian Sunday was born. For decades, perhaps many decades, the church observed both Sabbath and the Lord's Day. The day of rest and rejoicing in the gifts of God to Israel came more and more to be connected, understandably, with the special gift of God in Jesus as the Messiah, and thus the joys of Sabbath shifted to the Lord's Day. After the conversion of the Roman emperor Constantine to Christianity (312 AD), Christianity in time became the acknowledged religion of the empire. The Jewish Sabbath had long been recognized to be a rest day for the Jewish community in the empire; now Christianity too had its accepted holiday.

But would it be possible for the Christian Sunday to maintain the special character of the Jewish Sabbath? It would not be long before religious celebrations and ritual acts would claim much of the rest time of the Christian Sabbath, now the Lord's Day, Sunday. And so it has gone through the centuries: a day appointed for rest and relaxation, for reflection on life's meaning and purpose, for study and for enjoyment of family and friends, all too easily became a religious, ceremonial day—a time for worship that would of course be of critical importance for the life of faith. But lacking that special, central purpose of the Jewish Sabbath, the Lord's Day has all too frequently in Christian history become another workday—a day of religious labor, not just for priest and pastor, but for the entire congregation.

Is it possible for Christians to reclaim the gift of a seventh day of rest for rejoicing in the Lord? Such a reclaiming would not be easy, as we well know. The development of Saturday as a day of rest from labor and Sunday as the day for religious observance has been a good thing. The five-day week is surely a solid gain, a gain that is reported to be undergoing inroads these days. And for many in our secular world, the danger of losing the meaning of Sunday may be more grave than the danger of losing the meaning of the Sabbath. Both, we can safely say, are in danger.

Jewish observance of Sabbath has also had to contend with religious ceremonies that occupy much of the day. Sabbath rest can easily be crowded out by ceremonial religious observances, just as it has been in the Christian Sunday. What can be done? Both communities would benefit, I believe, by a fresh effort to reclaim Sabbath rest from all labor, including religious labor. But it should not be simply rest; it must be rest that enables, encourages, and is marked by genuine rejoicing in the Lord.

Some persons rest too much, as we noted. Others simply do not know how to rest at all. The individuals in the first group need a lesson in real rest, the kind of rest that God also enjoys. Those in the second group desperately need to be helped to stop their frenzied activity and do absolutely nothing for a time. The growth of retreat centers and other ways of reclaiming time for reflection and for companionship with God offers hope that Christians as well as Jews may again "remember the Sabbath day, and keep it holy."

Honoring Parents

It is easy to misread the intention of the fifth commandment. It is *not* addressed primarily to children. The Ten Commandments were addressed first of all to adult Israelites. Of course, the commandment applies to children as well as adults, but its first concern is to protect the entire family, all the generations that make up the family, from the youngest to the most aged.

What was the problem that the commandment sought to correct? It was the very problem that is always present in the family: how the generations were to treat one another. The ties of blood and kin that unite a family in love are intended to nurture and nourish all members, providing safety and security for all, enabling dependent young children to come to personal freedom and independence, and enabling adults to claim their mature place in the family as older adults move aside and give authority and responsibility to the generation behind them in age.

Who among us cannot recognize just how difficult it is for families to function in this intended, wholesome way? Children can easily be prevented from claiming their independence and full selfhood by (often unintentional) unwise and unhealthy parenting. Their safety and security are imperiled, as we know all too well, by predatory members of the family.

Similarly, adults often find that their parents are unable or unwilling to turn over responsibility for leadership in the family or in family enterprises to their children. What are adults to do when older adults, who are a huge percentage of the adult population today, cannot or will not accept their inability to maintain their former place within the family and the community?

The fifth commandment has in mind all these tensions, but it also has in mind the absolutely central place of this God-given institution— the family. The family gives us life, supports us in life, trains us for life, heals our wounds, eases our pain, loves and accepts us no matter what we do. Who can live without family? Even so, perhaps because of the closeness and the intimacy of family relationships, no wounds are so deep as those inflicted by loving/hating family members, no arguments so lasting and bitter as family arguments, and no exploitation so humiliating and unbearable as that by a family member. Small wonder that the commandment says, "Honor your father and your mother"!

Protecting the Family

Special laws such as Exodus 21:15 and 21:17 existed to protect the family, calling for the death penalty for anyone who struck down father or mother or pronounced curses on them. Legislation in the book of Deuteronomy, which often softens that found in Exodus, allows the community to stone a rebellious child to death when all other discipline has failed (Deut. 21:18–21). And there are similar laws dealing with sexual abuses within the family (Lev. 18; Lev. 20, for example).

This commandment offers a policy statement about life in the family. Like the other commandments, it provides help and guidance, not legislation. The commandment builds on a deep conviction about the value of life, a conviction that also underlies the next two commandments. This conviction is of bedrock importance for the Israelite community and is equally important for every society. Simply put: *God watches over human life as parents watch over their children.* The Bible speaks with special seriousness about widows and orphans, the outcast and the despised. For all of these, God is protector and parent and friend. But it is equally true that God watches over the family as a protector and parent and companion. Indeed, God is the head of the family.

Put another way, one may say that life belongs to God. It is God's gift, and it is God who demands that it be protected and nourished. A corollary of that understanding is clear: life does not grow in value as a child becomes an adult, and life does not lose value as adults become older adults. This last point is surely one of the major emphases of the fifth commandment: do not dishonor your aging parents!

Honoring Aged Parents Today

Could any more timely guideline for life be imagined? But how are we to apply the guideline? Nothing at all is gained by adding to the guilt of adult children who struggle to understand how best to help care for their aged parents. And certainly nothing is gained by encouraging aged parents to believe that their children are mistreating them, pushing them aside, treating them as worthless. Aging itself seems all too easily to lead to that conclusion. What, then, is the way to follow this fifth commandment?

At its heart, it simply offers a sound basic guideline: Be extremely careful as a member of the family that you do not damage this all-important resource of life and living. Remember that life is God's gift, a gift that God will not have treated lightly. Human beings are more than workers; they retain their full value when they no longer earn their keep. Children have equal value before they can pay their way; the elderly lose no value in retirement or when life slowly slips away.

Sabbath Rest for the Elderly

The two commandments we are looking at clearly belong together. Aged parents enter on their Sabbath rest. What a reminder to all to observe the Sabbath! All of us, if God gives us long life, have to stop working one day. For some retirees, ceasing from productive work is almost a death sentence. For others, of course, retirement means shirking all responsibility and entering the world of play and selfish indifference to the world's work and needs. We can be thankful that most active elderly seem able to avoid either extreme.

Old age also brings infirmities that often reduce drastically the quality of life. Here too the commandment has its word to speak. We never get so old or feeble that we no longer need companionship, loving care, the touch of another hand, words and song and music.

Just as God rests on the Sabbath, so God shares life with parents who seek to nourish and protect their family. God never gives up on a wayward child, and God never deserts the aged who feel themselves speeding toward death. To honor one's parents is also to honor God— the father and mother of us all.

Questions for Discussion

1. What might Christians today do to observe the Sabbath in healthy ways?
2. What does the commandment to honor parents suggest is the basis of what makes persons valuable?
3. What are the struggles we face in trying to honor our parents?

4

Protecting Life and Marriage

You shall not kill.
You shall not commit adultery.

—Exodus 20:13, 14

*T*he remaining five commandments all address issues that damage or even destroy life in community. Violence against individuals may end in their death. Violence against the sexual integrity of the family can damage or destroy family solidarity and stability. Stealing, false testimony before the authorities, and out-of-control envy of the life and fortunes of others can undermine the health of the society as a whole.

It may be helpful to distinguish the first two of these commandments from the remaining three. The first two prohibit violence against individuals, although of course the community is affected as well. The other three clearly have the larger community more directly in view. For that reason we deal with commandments six and seven together and then address the remaining three together.

The sixth and seventh commandments are flat and uncompromising prohibitions. Killing and adultery are ruled out, period! Earlier commandments offered comments and explanations; these offer nothing but the blunt prohibitions: killing and adultery are out.

Questions, of course, remain. What kind of killing is intended? All taking of human life, no matter what the circumstances? The Old Testament surely has a lot of killing recorded in it, and some of it is said to have been at God's direction. We saw above that there are laws calling for the execution of those who maim or curse their parents and of children who are uncontrollably rebellious. And yet, the commandment rules out killing! Similarly, adultery seems not to have meant in the biblical world what it means in our day. For men, adultery is having sexual relations with the fiancé or wife of another man. For women, however, it means having sexual relations with anyone other than one's fiancé or husband. These apparently clear and uncompromising commandments have to be unpacked and sorted out.

Kill or Murder?

Recent English translations of the sixth commandment seem clearly to prefer "murder" over "kill," thus moving away from long tradition in English versions of the Bible.[1] It is true that the Hebrew term *ratsach* is not the regular word for homicide. Its uses carry some flavor of intentional killing or even premeditation. At the same time, there are instances in which the word clearly does not mean murder in any sense of the term. Especially in connection with cities of refuge, the term is used to refer to killing that is specifically said *not* to be premeditated. Why, then, have translators turned to the more limited term? We will examine this question below.

The prohibition of adultery rests on an understanding of women, married and unmarried, as so strictly under the care and responsibility of their fathers or husbands as to count as the father's or husband's possession, his property. Viewed in this light, one might conclude that the prohibition of adultery bore close resemblance to the command against stealing. It would be a mistake, however, to let the cultural differences between the biblical world and our world—important though of course they are—mislead us. We need to keep these two commandments in their full force, in my judgment, choosing the more rigorous interpretation of both of them first and seeing where that decision leads us. I prefer to see the sixth commandment as a commandment against killing and to explore what that might mean for our day. Similarly, I prefer to see the commandment against adultery to include both men and women and to apply to both equally.

Restrictions on Killing in the Bible

The first killing recorded in the Bible, Cain's deliberate murder of his brother, Abel (Gen. 4), offers a restriction on the taking of human life. In response to Cain's plea that his sentence of banishment is unbearable, which would surely mean his death, he is given a protective mark of some kind, indicating that Cain has the protection of YHWH. By contrast, Lamech, Cain's descendant, boasts of taking vengeance on his enemies almost without limit (Gen. 4:23–24). The law of retaliation (*lex talionis*), an eye for an eye and a tooth for a tooth (Exod. 21:23–25), is a safeguard against excessive revenge taking such as that of Lamech. Again, there is a restriction on the taking of human life.

The most important such restriction in the book of Genesis appears in chapter nine. God's provisions for Noah's life in the new world following the great flood includes provision for the taking of animal life as food. This ancient poem contains a remarkable line: "Whoever sheds the blood of a human, by a human shall that person's blood be shed; for in his own image God made humankind." Animal life may be taken for food, but the lifeblood must be drained out to give due honor to the life force present in animals. The life of human beings, however, is God's creation; human beings, male and female, are created in God's image and likeness, and only God may authorize the taking of human life. This poem must surely have been the controlling image in early Israel.

Ironically, this ancient poem authorizes the human community to act in God's behalf in the taking of human life. Even so, only God can give the order.

Elaborate procedures were adopted for the protection of human life, and especially for miscarriages of justice. Already in early Israelite legislation (Exod. 21:12–14), provision is made for a killer who did not intend murder. Such killers could make their way to an altar and there claim asylum (see 1 Kgs. 1:49–53, for example). Later, cities of refuge are appointed that serve the same end. The taking of life, though allowed in specific instances, is directly under the oversight of God, whose kinship with all human beings, even murderers, must be remembered and observed.

Dilemmas for Israel and for Us

The dilemma is clear: Life belongs to God. Should any Israelite dare to take human life, God required that the community take the life of the killer. To safeguard human life, human life has to be taken. Some human beings care nothing about God's gift of life or God's commitment to protect life. How else can the community act than to step in and take the killer's life in return? Indeed, God requires such action.

The biblical instances in which the death penalty is introduced have led translators of the Bible to opt for the translation "murder" instead of "kill." That is an unwise move, as a recent writing has argued persuasively. Wilma Ann Bailey points out the limitations of the use of the term "murder," which means so many different things in the laws of various countries, and even in our different states. Moreover, the use of the more restrictive term draws the teeth from the prohibition. Of course God condemns murder; who doesn't? This is a commandment about the sanctity of life as such, and the dilemmas it brings will not be eased by the translation of the Hebrew term by the too restrictive term "murder."[2]

The dilemma is as old as human civilization and it will not go away. But situations do change. Earlier societies had no reliable penal system on the basis of which those bent on destroying human life could be restrained permanently but not put to death. Almost all societies in the developed world have eliminated the death penalty, counting on imprisonment to protect the society. The United States is a notorious exception. Many states have reintroduced the death penalty in recent years, and our courts continue to uphold the death penalty except in very special cases.

Many today find the continued execution of fellow human beings intolerable, even in our violent world. Repudiation of the death penalty would leave many dilemmas, but it would remove one. Perhaps no one can know with confidence whether the use of capital punishment is a deterrent against crime, as many claim it to be. There is no doubt whatever, however, that the death penalty is applied unfairly in our country, with African Americans and other minorities executed in disproportion to their numbers and to the nature of their crimes. With DNA testing, we are learning about more and more persons condemned to death and, in many instances, executed, who have been found to be not guilty of the crime for which they were convicted. And finally, while some societies might find it difficult to keep those bent on destroying life permanently imprisoned, our country is surely not one of them.

What of Abortion?

Perhaps no moral question more sharply divides our country's population than that of a woman's right to choose whether to bear children or not to do so. While this question has polarized the society and brought about fanatical and criminal acts by some of the parties involved, the discussion has had its great value. Who among us would today speak of abortion casually, suggesting that it is no moral problem at all? Who would say that human tissue that has not come to independent life through normal birth processes is of no moral concern whatever? Our society is much more ready today, I believe, to acknowledge that all living human tissue—from unused eggs, fertilized or not, to body parts left over from anatomy classes—deserves respectful attention and treatment. Those who uphold the right of women to decide whether they will or will not bear a child are well aware that the issue is a moral one, not just the individual's own business alone.

The rhetoric dealing with abortion is entirely unhelpful. Those who believe that human life begins with conception and plead and work against abortion surely know that those who support the right of women to decide whether and when to bear children are not murderers—deliberate, premeditated killers bent on callous destruction of life. And those who are for women's rights know that those who cannot endure to see living tissue discarded are not all religious fanatics and enemies of human freedom and responsible childbearing. The dilemma is inescapable. Choices are sometimes heartbreaking: shall the child be carried to term when it is known, known without doubt, that nothing like a normal life for the child is physically possible? If the conditions of life are so lean and grim that another child will threaten the life of the entire family, does one dare to bring another life into the world?

Pacifism

Pacifists throughout the centuries have insisted that the taking of human life is intolerable, no matter what the offenders may have done. With great persuasion they argue that retaliation against violent acts must not repeat the violence. In order to break the dreadful circle of violence, some must flatly refuse to take human life or be directly complicit in doing so. The "peace churches" are the most notable examples, Mennonites and Quakers being the best known. The cost of the pacifist witness is high indeed, but its benefits for the larger society, in my judgment, are enormous. Never was this witness more severely tested than in the time of national socialism's deliberate and "scientific" program to exterminate every Jew living in Europe simply for being a Jew—and Jews had no right to exist, according to this despicable philosophy. How was it possible to hold to one's pacifist position in the face of such public, grotesque evil? Pacifists sought ways to do their duty as citizens short of taking up arms against fellow human beings, even in face of such violence. And, in more recent years, monstrous tribal and ethnic slaughter has posed similar issues for those who simply cannot deliberately engage in acts of violence against fellow human beings.

The majority position of religious communities, rightly or wrongly, has followed the guidelines of Genesis 9:6, taking on themselves the awesome responsibility to act in God's behalf to stop the taking of human life *precisely in order to preserve human life.*

Life and Death with Dignity

Another form of the dilemma has become more evident in recent decades as the life span of persons in the developed countries has greatly increased. There is much discussion of the *quality* of life that remains in the case of a person who continues to have a kind of life that can hardly be called life at all. Does there come a time when extraordinary interventions to keep heart and lungs working is not only unnecessary but wrong? Again, family and friends may find themselves driven to accept the taking of the life of a loved one in order to preserve and protect the dignity and the very selfhood of the dying person.

Death with dignity has a corollary, too often overlooked. God's creatures are also entitled to life with dignity. The Ten Commandments seek to uphold the right to life with dignity, in my judgment. What a responsibility that understanding places on communities, governments, and individuals! The commandment not to kill, if extended to the preservation of all living tissue, ought certainly be extended to include life with dignity for all of those whom God has created in the divine image and likeness. Are God's creatures living dignified lives when they are deprived of the most elemental necessities of life—food and drink and clothing and meaningful labor? Is earth's population treated with dignity when a small percentage of the population consumes the major portion of earth's resources, and a scandalously large percentage of earth's peoples struggle to live with dignity while unable to feed and clothe their children or offer them hope for the future?

Conditions of life have much to do with the very continuance of life. What a dilemma all this poses for those of us who enjoy earth's goods, even when we work valiantly in behalf of those who have much less of God's abundance than do we!

One hopeful development in the face of these dilemmas is, I believe, the great increase in the spread of information. The gap between rich and poor can no longer pass unnoticed. No longer do impoverished communities and individuals know simply that some neighbors nearby have much more than they have. Virtually all of earth's population today knows about the gap between rich and poor, privileged and underprivileged, those able to care for their basic needs and those who simply cannot do so. To the extent that it is within the power of those of us with more than we need to help those with less than they need, does not the commandment "You shall not kill" require of us that we do so? One thing the information revolution has brought to pass: the rest of the world knows in some detail whether we are sharing our goods and supporting life as we should, or are simply content to let the disparity between our quality of life and that of the majority of earth's peoples continue unchallenged. How could we be surprised if there are violent reactions?

The biblical command does not provide a clear answer to the above dilemmas, of course. Its basic value, I believe, is that it registers one central affirmation: life belongs to God. Any taking of life must be done with awareness that the life taken is God's creation, God's gift, and precious in God's sight. Do those taking the life recognize that in doing so they are acting in God's stead? Are they able to live with that recognition? Some will surely continue to find it impossible to accept that responsibility. Others will accept that responsibility; one may hope that they do so only because they are convinced that no alternative is better able, in the given circumstances, to preserve more life than is taken.

"You Shall Not Commit Adultery"

The commandment against adultery has a clear aim. It is intended to protect the family in general, and in particular to safeguard the betrothal and marriage of daughters. While a prophet could condemn even King David for his adultery with Bathsheba (2 Sam. 12), the commandment was more restrictive on engaged or married women. Ancient Israel gave more sexual latitude to males than to females, since tribal and ethnic identity were more easily traceable through the mother, but also because of the favored position of males within the society. Sexual relations by a man with unengaged or unmarried women other than his wife or wives apparently were not actual violations of the commandment. For women, however, sexual relations with anyone other than the betrothed or the husband were acts of adultery. Moreover, sexual activity before engagement or marriage would eliminate or at least greatly reduce any prospect of a woman's securing a proper husband. The father of a woman was the guarantor that his daughter came to the marriage as a virgin (see Deut. 22). The inequality is twofold: men might have more than one wife, and men's sexual activity was much less restricted than that of women.

The critical importance of children to a household, of course, helps to explain the presence of polygamy. Barrenness is often listed as the cause of the taking of a second wife. Kings and potentates, of course, were exceptions. They were larger than life and their actions exceeded those of ordinary folk. The biblical ideal is, unmistakably, monogamy, as is clear from Genesis 2. The most likely reading of that chapter sees God's act of building the first woman from the rib of the first 'adham (humanoid?) ending with the creation of a male and a female at once, each dependent on the other for the completion of the existence of both. Should a man take a second wife, even if the first wife was bought as a slave, the man was obligated to see to it that both wives were treated equally in every way (Exod. 21:7–11).

Implications of the Commandment against Adultery

This commandment does not prohibit all sexual relations outside marriage, as we have seen. Implicit, however, in the biblical stories and teachings about human sexuality is one central point: human sexuality is a good gift of a good God, designed to bring pleasure to the partners and also to assure a next generation of human beings on God's earth. Genesis 1 includes God's blessing on human beings, male and female, and God's command that they enjoy the blessing of sexual relations and populate the earth. Genesis 2 reveals the delight with which the first man greets the first woman: "This at last is bone of my bones and flesh of my flesh" (Gen. 2:23). Sarah can speak with incredulity when promised a child in her old age, saying in effect: "Shall I have fun with my husband, old as I am?" (Gen. 18:12). And Jesus' first miracle is at a wedding feast at Cana (John 2).

Also implicit in the commandment is the condemnation of sexual violence of all kinds. But does the Bible perhaps go even farther? The very act itself, according to some texts, makes the two partners one. Most remarkable is the apostle Paul's insistence to the church at Corinth that sexual relations between a man and a prostitute creates a union; they become one flesh! (1 Cor. 6:12–20). What a teaching, especially by one who is not praised for his teaching about human sexuality or the value of marriage! Paul's reference to Genesis 2 is sound, I believe: the sexual act both brings into being a union of the two partners, and creates the possibility of a new generation of human beings. Individuals who come together sexually may produce children, but whether they do or not, their coming together creates a "new thing in the world," as Jeremiah describes it in an enigmatic statement (Jer. 31:22).

On this view, biblical sexual teaching may offer its most important teaching for our day and for any day. Do not suppose, the Bible may be implying, that there is such a thing as sex without consequences. The act itself changes things. Not only does a virgin cease to be a virgin. The first sexual act and all subsequent acts bring two persons together in such intimacy that both are changed, different, bound to one another (whether they wish it or not) by the act itself. And the union has two specific aims: to enrich the life of both partners, and to contribute something to the next generation.

Such a view of sexual relations might suggest, then, that the commandment against adultery is by implication a prohibition of sexual relations outside engagement and marriage. Does such teaching offer any help at all to our world? I believe that it offers critically important help.

Even if persons believe that sexual relations outside the bonds of marriage are acceptable, they can learn from the Bible that every sexual engagement creates a unity. To accept the view that sex produces such a unity is surely to rule out sexual conquests, going from partner to partner, even if one finds one willing partner after another. It is also to rule out any notion that sexual relations are without consequences— perhaps only emotional, but perhaps moral, economic, and spiritual consequences.

One additional matter has to be addressed: the Bible's words about homosexuality. The first thing to say is that there are only five such texts: Leviticus 18:22; 20:13; Romans 1:27; 1 Corinthians 6:9; and 1 Timothy 1:9–10. Not one of these texts has in view lifetime commitments in love between persons of the same gender, commitments that abound in our world and are entirely unrelated to the exploitative sexual relations referred to in the Bible. It is a travesty of biblical interpretation to claim these five texts as warrant for the condemnation of all such loving commitments of gays and lesbians today. It is quite another thing, of course, to condemn exploitative sexual relations, heterosexual and homosexual, that abound also in our world. Such relations should be condemned; they violate all aspects of the Bible's depiction of the God-given bond of sexual union that changes the partners, brings them joy, and contributes life and blessing to the next generation.

The Bible knows the mystery and power of sexual attraction. King David's son Amnon (2 Sam. 13) becomes physically ill due to his lust for his sister, and he spurns her with revulsion once he has raped her. The depths of sexual attraction, wholesome and perverse, seem to lie beyond our plumbing. Small wonder that religious ecstasy and sexual ecstasy have often been compared—and confused! Just as fervent devotion to God can all too easily lead to fanaticism, so also passionate engagement in the mystery of sex can all too easily lead to exploitation and abuse. Must it always be so, as that old popular song by the Mills Brothers put it, that "You always hurt the one you love"?

Questions for Discussion

1. Recent English translations of the sixth commandment seem to prefer the term "murder" instead of "kill." What issues does that raise?
2. What might be some practical applications of the principle of taking human life only to preserve human life?
3. What implications do you see in the commandment against adultery?

5

Ensuring Wholesome Life
in Community

You shall not steal.
You shall not bear false witness against your neighbor.
You shall not covet your neighbor's house.
　　　　　　　　　　　　　　　　　—Exodus 20:15–17

*T*he last three commandments also belong together. They rule
out major threats to the society. While applicable of course to
individuals, they identify activities of both individuals and
groups that, when rampant, threaten the very life of a community and a society. These offenses against the community also
have a way of corrupting the lives and actions of otherwise
decent and responsible persons. Enshrined in the institutions of
a community, they corrupt the entire community.

Do Not Steal

The first of the three, "Do not steal," is as brief and pointed as
the commandments against killing and adultery. Again, however, things aren't quite as direct and clear as they appear. Scholars have pointed out that the last of the commandments, "Do not
covet," must surely point to forbidden *actions*, not just attitudes
or intentions. How could the community possibly enforce
wrong desires or the like? The tenth commandment, they say,
must therefore be talking about desiring the life or goods of others and *setting out to secure them.*

　　The commandment against stealing, they say, would then have
a very specific kind of stealing in view: the stealing of human

beings, in particular the stealing of slaves. See Deuteronomy 23:15–16, which prohibits the return of a runaway slave, demanding rather that the community make a place for the one who has gained freedom.

This view is wrong, in my judgment. The command against stealing is broad and far-reaching, just as the other commandments are. Moreover, as we shall point out in discussing the tenth commandment, the more probable meaning of that commandment is precisely to resist being overcome with desire for the life and goods of others. Coveting is indeed an activity, an activity of the soul, of the inner being of a person. And as we have noted in the first chapter, these commandments are not legislation but policy statements, demands that depend for their effectiveness on a commitment of the heart and soul, not on threats of punishment or specific laws.

The commandment does indeed have in mind the stealing of the life of persons as well as their belongings. When anyone or any institution takes away the life, the selfhood, the honor, or the goods of others, that is stealing, and the eighth commandment says, "No!" The prophet Amos denounced those who would "sell the righteous for silver, and the needy for a pair of sandals" (Amos 2:6). The book of Exodus even prohibits taking someone's cloak as security for a debt and keeping it overnight: how can one live without cover for the night? (Exod. 22:26–27).

It may be difficult for some of us who live in countries surfeited with goods and plagued by efforts to sell us yet more goods to realize just what value a single item might have in a household living at the very margin of existence. The reference to keeping a man's cloak overnight reveals this difference between our society and that of the biblical writer. The text indicates that one cloak per person, doing duty as cover during cold days and every night, was all too common. Or think of the theft of one's donkey or ox, or one's household knife. The loss of one such possession would be a catastrophe almost as severe as the losses that we might suffer in a tornado or a hurricane, in all probability.

History is full of instances of those with more of earth's goods than they could ever use or need exacting severe penalties against those who dare to take anything from that excess. We all know the difference between a person's stealing food to keep the children alive and making one's living through a life of crime—whether as a housebreaker or as a corrupt financial adviser, politician, or retailer. Amos also spoke about those who made "the ephah small and the shekel great," using false measures and weights in their shops (Amos 8:5). Nevertheless, both kinds of activity are stealing, and the commandment condemns both.

Other Kinds of Stealing

Countries living in affluence are increasingly aware of other situations to which the commandment applies. When a particular community or country or group of countries claims for itself the right to overuse the limited goods of the planet, is that not stealing from those who deserve a more nearly equitable share of these gifts of God? Once more, the prophet Amos shames and condemns us:

> Alas for those who lie on beds of ivory,
>   and lounge on their couches,
> and eat lambs from the flock,
>   and calves from the stall; . . .
> who drink wine from bowls,
>   and anoint themselves with the finest oils,
>   but are not grieved over the ruin of Joseph!
>   (Amos 6:4–6)

Nothing is gained, of course, by merely adding to the guilt that decent people feel about the disparity between their affluent life and the plight of the poor. If the commandment leads citizens and their leaders to use every opportunity to reduce the obscene imbalance between the lives of rich and poor, that is an enormous gain. And, following Amos, we guilty ones can at the least cry out against the imbalance and keep calling for change.

When workers fail to render a day's work for a day's pay, they steal from their employers. When employers fail to provide fair payment and fair benefits for workers, they steal from their employees. When teachers fail to provide students with their best instruction, they steal from those students. When lobbyists unduly influence legislators or others to support damaging policies, they and their employees steal from the public. "You shall not steal" is a commandment that applies over the entire sweep of a society's social, economic, and cultural activities.

Another form of stealing is related to unfair consumption of earth's goods. Each generation is responsible for its custody of earth's goods and opportunities during its own span of life. Is it not also responsible to keep in view the generations that lie ahead? Poor stewards steal from the current generation, but they also steal from the generation to come. Think of fossil fuels that are consumed as though there were no tomorrow! Think of the unique Amazon forest and other rain forests being gobbled up for profit. The prophet Isaiah spoke about those who "join house to house, who add field to field," until there is room for no one but them in the land (Isa. 5:8). Visions of equal sharing of earth's goods and rational means for securing the life of generations to come on the planet may be no more than visions. We should remember, however, that we are guided and empowered by visions—visions enable us to do better than we would do without them.

What, then, is stealing? It is *any activity that damages or destroys a person's or a community's opportunity for a tolerable life in community—consisting at least of adequate food, clothing, shelter, work, and hope for the future.*

Bearing False Witness

The ninth commandment is not about lying, whether the kindly kind of lie or the malice-laden lie. The Bible has lots to say about lying, of course—particularly in the books of Proverbs and James. But this commandment has a particular kind of falsehood in view: *public testimony before the judges or the elders on the basis of which the community's leaders can uphold justice and maintain healthy institutions.* Of course, it applies to the individual's speaking the truth and avoiding slander, but its focus is on the machinery by which a society deals fairly and honorably with its citizens. When the instruments of justice cannot be trusted, public confidence in government declines or disappears. The result is chaos, or a reign of terror.

The third commandment and the ninth are related, but they are clearly distinct. The third commandment aims at the health of the religious institutions and all processes by which a community and its individuals seek to draw close to God. Taking God's name in vain is using the special gifts of God to serve selfish ends or do violence to our neighbors and enemies. The ninth commandment also deals with the power of human speech, but its direction is horizontal, not vertical. Can one count on the structures by which communities can live together in harmony to treat all fairly? Will the police let racial prejudice lead them to shade their testimony in favor of whites? or against homosexuals? or in support of the rich and powerful at the expense of the poor and the powerless?

The reach of the commandment is much wider still. Will scholars and teachers use their sources and their knowledge faithfully and responsibly, or will they be led to false testimony out of laziness or a desire to secure their positions of authority? Will advertisers, charged to put the best possible "spin" on their products, deliberately mislead the public? Will political leaders withhold information that does damage to their cause by shading the information they share? Will preachers steal from other preachers or from Internet resources and represent the stolen items as their own? Will gossipers go so far as to damage or destroy their neighbors, not so much out of malice as simply because gossiping is fun?

What does this commandment have as its aim? *A wholesome and healthy life in community, where fellow human beings live together peaceably, avoiding deliberate harm to one another and to the institutions that make the lives of all more manageable and pleasant.* It is a good thing indeed that we have checks and balances, procedures that help us to help one another to speak the truth in love to one another and to uphold the truth zealously in our public forums.

Some biblical texts well illustrate the long efforts in Israel to uphold truth telling. One safeguard was the requirement that in capital cases a single witness did not suffice; there must be at least two or three (Deut. 17:6). More important were the marvelous instances of the corrupting influence of false testimony. In the days of King Ahab and Queen Jezebel, a property owner named Naboth, who would not sell his land to the king, was put to death on the evidence of two witnesses who had been ordered by the queen to accuse Naboth falsely (1 Kgs. 21). A memorable story from the earliest days of the Christian church is recorded in Acts 5. Some early Christians were selling property in order to contribute to the needs of the Christian community in the Jerusalem area. A man named Ananias and his wife Sapphira did so as well, but they testified before the community that the property had sold for less than its actual selling price. They were condemned, and they fell down dead (Acts 5:1–11). The lie, said the apostle Peter, was not to the apostles, but to God.

Lying and stealing are often intermingled. One lies in order to get away with stealing, but false testimony also robs the community of trustworthy institutions and the sense of public confidence that they produce. Once lost, such public trust is very difficult to regain. In our country the widespread deplorable loss of confidence in public officials has brought great damage to all the institutions of government. The slogan "The less government, the better" is a dangerous outcome of such public mistrust. The often-repeated statement that when a state legislature completes its annual or biennial session and goes home, citizens can breathe a sigh of relief, reflects this damaging mistrust.

You Shall Not Covet Your Neighbor's House

The meaning of the tenth commandment is much discussed and disputed, as we noted above.[1] Does it really have in mind an attitude, a disposition, a kind of deep envy of the fortunes of others? If so, does that not make this commandment differ entirely from the others? Some interpreters think that the verb translated "covet" must surely mean more than an attitude or a disposition. Does it not rather mean "take steps to seize" or some such action?

One strong reason for insisting on the translation "covet" is the parallel passage in Deuteronomy 5:21. The passage gives as a parallel meaning for "covet," a Hebrew term meaning "desire." What could be plainer? The term for "covet" appears in only one other place in the Hebrew Bible—Micah 2:2—where again the evidence supports the translation "covet." That passage reads, "They [that is, the condemned evildoers] covet fields, and seize them; houses, and take them away." The term's meaning is clear, I believe. The tenth commandment speaks against, not just ordinary envy, but an almost obsessive desire for the life and property of others. It is therefore a good counterpart to the eighth commandment, "You shall not steal." Not only must one not take the life or goods of another person; one must not, for one's own sake, let the imbalances and injustices of life sicken one and drive one to inappropriate action.

The critics who insist that the term must refer to actual movement toward taking the life or goods of others are right to this extent: the commandment does constitute an action. But it is an action within the soul, the self, the inner being of persons who are sickened with longing for that which others have. Whole industries today are devoted to bringing that sickness upon us. Ingenious and repetitive bombardment of persons with images of the way others live are inescapable in the developed world, and they are increasingly a part of the daily fare of others far removed from societies surfeited with goods. Those who say that the translation "covet" helps to support the present scandalous imbalance between the haves and the have-nots fail to recognize that the kind of sick longing for the life and goods of others affects all persons, including those who have everything. The sickness can easily become a gnawing desire for *more*—not necessarily more of a given item or treatment or plaudit, but just *more*. The driving force in the lives of powerful and wealthy and successful folk, it seems, is often just this desire for more. Who has not met the person who, having been awarded many prizes or medals, yearns and strives and even schemes for more? Overachievers are likely to be touched by this sickness.

It is just this hankering after more than one needs or can use that often leads to stealing, to acting on the perverse desire. But even when the coveting is not acted on, the destructive effects take their toll. Those who covet can never be content with what they have, with what they have been given, or what they have earned. It is never enough.

Coveting is not restricted to any group or any social or economic class. It is a sickness akin to the impulses that lead to destructive or violent behavior. It is a sickness of the soul, affecting everyone, but affecting some persons so deeply that their lives are sickened, soured, spoiled.

Is there any cure? How does one seek to resist coveting? The first word of counsel is to recognize that one need not look at the coveting of others; the problem is one's own. How do I address my coveting the reputation, the prizes won, the contracts landed, the raises received, the children born, the general good fortune of my neighbors?

I know of no better counsel than that of Jesus to the rich young man who came asking what he needed to do to inherit eternal life (Mark 10:17 and parallels). Give to the poor! Envy of those who have more than we have can be confronted best by sharing our abundance with those who have a right to envy us for what we have!

But, finally, the best response may be the pious and sobering conclusion to which the author of Psalm 73 comes. After having powerfully portrayed the prosperity of evildoers in the world and after having honestly acknowledged how the prosperity of the wicked was almost the author's undoing, this poet finally comes to inquire what is the most precious reality in all the world. The answer is quite simply: God's presence, God's intimate holding of the hand, and the promise that this divine presence is permanent. The psalmist, rightly, closes with an affirmation that God does see to justice in the world; justice and equality are never ignored or forgotten. Even so, God's nearness—that is the highest treasure. Is there any better antidote to crippling envy than the recognition that what one most wants in all the world is confidence in life's meaning, in a future that transcends physical death, in a life with God?

Questions for Discussion

1. How might the commandment against stealing speak to behaviors across contemporary society?
2. Why is the prohibition against bearing false witness so crucial to the health of a community?
3. Why are people so prone to covet what others have? How can we resist this sickness of the soul?

6

Keeping the Commandments

The word is very near to you; it is in your mouth and in your heart for you to observe.
—Deuteronomy 30:14

Oh, how I love your law!
—Psalm 119:97

Love Is the Context

The Ten Commandments are set in the context of God's love and mercy. God heard the outcry of oppressed people in Egypt and sent Moses and Aaron to lead them to freedom. The context of the divine demands is God's love—a point underscored, as we noted, by the prologue: "I am the LORD your God, who brought you out of the land of Egypt, out of the house of slavery" (Exod. 20:2). It should be no surprise, then, if Israel's attitude toward the commandments is marked by joy and thankfulness.

Praise and Gratitude

Have you noticed how difficult it is for some persons to give gifts freely and accept them properly? Giving and receiving gifts in a wholesome way is a challenge—a challenge, it seems, for all gift givers and receivers. All too often, the *attitude* of one or both spoils the gift and damages the relationship.

On the part of the giver, too often strings are attached. The gift is not freely given, for the donor specifies—sometimes in great detail—just how the gift is to be used. Charitable gifts to institutions may rightly be designated for specific purposes, of course, but gifts that are designed to help regulate the recipient's *conduct* are problematic indeed. An aunt, for example, may give gifts to her nieces and nephews and never tire of reminding the recipients of the gifts, expecting a lifetime of appreciation, attention, and adulation.

On the part of the receiver of gifts, attitude is critical. Three all too frequent feelings show up in gift exchanges between loved ones. The nieces and nephews who receive the aunt's largess may resent their gift deeply: Why should *she* have all that money in the first place? And who is she to try to run our lives? Or, on the contrary, they may lavish praise and attention on the aunt, paving the way for more gifts, losing all dignity and self-respect in the process. Or—perhaps worst of all—they may complacently receive the gift, confident that the aunt did just the right thing. Why wouldn't she be generous to such fine persons as we are?

On God's part, the gift of Torah was surely made with strings attached. Note, however, that the kinds of conduct that are ruled out open up a vast arena of free choice for Israel. The prohibitions mean life and blessing for Israel; Israel is invited to accept them—and live! (Deut. 30:15–20). No complacency is in order, according to the book of Deuteronomy, for Israel was far from being the most noble or the strongest or the wisest or the most morally upright of earth's nations when God chose it (see Deut. 7, 8, and 9).

But how easy it was for Israel to respond to the gift in damaging and unworthy ways! Complacency about God's gift of Torah was entirely inappropriate, for Israel was not the most righteous of nations (Deut. 9:4–5), then or later on. Sullen resentment that the path of faithfulness was too hard is also ruled out, for the commandments are possible to keep (Deut. 30:11–14). And God does not want fawning adoration or lavish gifts and offerings, but faithful service, a kindly spirit, and loving devotion (Mic. 6:6–8).

Praising God is different from thanking God. The nieces and nephews can tell their aunt how wonderful she is and how much they love her without resentment or servility or complacency. Israel can do the same. Love for God expressed in acts of praise and deeds of love and mercy rightly acknowledge the gift and the Giver.

Much of the life of prayer, I believe, is marred by our difficulty in rendering praise and proper thanksgiving to God. How easy it is to grovel and plead, to confess our unworthiness to receive God's favor and blessing because of our sins—as though we were the worst sinners in all the world! The truth, no doubt, is that we are just ordinary sinners who also are creatures created in God's image and pronounced to be good. Or, on the contrary, how easy it is to feel resentment that God seems not to come to our aid, treats us unfairly by comparison with the lives of others, or keeps poking a divine finger into our affairs! The book of Job shows what it feels like to have been singled out, it seemed, for every punishment that earth or God could inflict. Job can ask simply to be left alone with his spittle! (Job 7:19).[1] And, sad to say, some Christians (I won't speak for Jews) seem entirely content to believe that their good fortune is well deserved and the very least that God could do for such good folk as they are.

These problems vanish when we simply praise God for our lives and for all that we receive from God's hands, a gift of love for One we love with all of our being. Love is the motivator of praise and thanksgiving, and love defies explanation or justification; it is the greatest gift and the greatest mystery of life.

Jewish and Christian Perspectives on Law

"The Old Testament is a book of law; the New Testament is a book of grace." How many times I have heard that observation—and how wrong it is, on both counts! As we have noted earlier, Israelite law is placed in the context of God's love and mercy. And the New Testament could hardly be more emphatic than it is in laying down the strict demands of what Jesus called the kingdom of God or the kingdom of heaven. The two Testaments agree fully that God's love and grace entail demands, and that the demands spring from divine love and mercy.

Even so, the term *torah*, which means "teaching," "guidance," or "instruction," is a dominant reality for Israel and for the Jewish community today. "The Torah" can refer most narrowly to the Ten Commandments themselves, or more broadly to the legal materials of the first five books of the Old Testament, or to the first five books of the Old Testament as a whole, or to the entire Hebrew Bible. We could say that when a Jew says, "The Torah says," he or she means just about what a Christian means when he or she says, "The Bible says."

Christians speak much more of God's love and grace, displayed in the life, deeds, teaching, suffering, death, and resurrection of Jesus. Jesus demonstrates God's love for all people and invites all to receive that love and live by its power. But the living out of God's gift of love involves fidelity to Jesus' way of displaying and demonstrating God's love for all—and that means what Paul calls "the law of Christ" (Gal. 6:2).

Scholars debate what the apostle Paul meant by his sharp contrast between law and gospel in the books of Galatians and Romans. Surely the emphasis is on the contrast between trusting in one's own righteousness and trusting in God's forgiving love in Christ. Faithful service to Torah did not mean trusting in one's own righteousness, not at all. It meant accepting God's gracious gift of deliverance from bondage and binding oneself to the demands of God's covenant of love. The parable of the Pharisee and the tax collector (Luke 18:9–14) makes the point vividly, although the use of the term "Pharisee" has caused misunderstanding. Pharisees in Jesus' day were among the most faithful and helpful interpreters of Torah as a gift of love and grace. Some Pharisees, no doubt, like some Christians throughout the centuries, in their zeal for Torah turned it into an oppressive burden—precisely because they let the connection between love and law slip away. Both Torah and the Christian gospel can be interpreted and presented legalistically and without love or grace. The result is a harsh, joyless, praiseless Judaism or Christianity—a caricature of the true character of both.

Law and Freedom

The negative form of the commandments is misleading. The fact that the commandments are primarily negative in form does not mean that they express a negative attitude toward life and the world. Far from it!

Like many policy statements in legal documents, they are put negatively, leaving open a whole arena of freedom and open possibility. For example, the First Amendment to the U.S. Constitution includes the famous statement, "Congress shall make no law respecting an establishment of religion, or prohibiting the free exercise thereof." That clause contains specific restrictions on the Congress, but it leaves open an enormously wide range of freedom to Congress and to the citizens of the United States. Two things are not allowed: establishing one religion as the religion of the land, and restricting in any way the free exercise of religion. Citizens are free to worship God as they see fit, just as they are free not to worship God at all. Congress is not at liberty to declare Christianity the religion of the land, but surely some freedom remains for Congress to act in ways that might support general religious concerns, so long as it does not favor one religion over another. We will discuss one area of possible governmental freedom below, when we deal with the much-debated question of the posting of the Ten Commandments in public places.

There is another dimension to the freedom implied in policy prohibitions like the Ten Commandments. Take, for example, the commandment to "remember" or "observe" the Sabbath. Probably this commandment once read, "Do not dishonor the sabbath," or perhaps, "Do not work on the sabbath [seventh] day." The prohibitions of the Ten Commandments invite and demand discussion, debate—a continuing debate over the years and the centuries—as to just what the prohibition means for a given generation. Think of the changes that have occurred in the interpretation and application of this commandment over the centuries! Such debates are the lifeline of morality in a society. There is no fixed and unalterable interpretation of the commandments; rather, there is an inescapable demand that the meaning of the commandments be debated and reviewed over time.

To continue with the prohibition of work on the Sabbath: What is the central or core purpose of that commandment? It is, as we noted above, to assure that a healthy rhythm of work and rest from work is maintained. It is intended to assure that human beings and other living beings not have the life squeezed out of them by excessive labor. It is to assure that children are not doomed to do adult labor and thereby be deprived of a childhood.

Similarly, the flat commandment not to kill opens up a vast arena of human freedom that must be claimed and used responsibly. The core prohibition in this case is unmistakable: life is precious to God and it must be precious to us, God's creatures. But how are we best to honor God's commitment to life? As we noted above, it is sometimes apparently necessary to take life in order to save life. But there are daily decisions that enable us freely to choose how to honor life: by how we treat our bodies, by how we treat our neighbors, by how we support policies designed to assure some minimum of life's possible benefits for all our fellow citizens, and by how we speak and think and write of warfare and terrorism in a time when emotions run high.

The commandment not to kill casts a spotlight on many aspects of our private and public lives, showing us unmistakably what we are doing to damage life and what we are doing to enhance life. And that is liberating!

But Can We Keep the Law?

Now we come to a question that would appear to divide Jews and Christians. The book of Deuteronomy underscores the "keepability" of God's Torah, God's Law. The apostle Paul speaks for many Christians when he says,

> For I delight in the law of God in my inmost self, but I see in my members another law at war with the law of my mind, making me captive to the law of sin that dwells in my members. Wretched man that I am! Who will rescue me from this body of death? (Rom. 7:22–24)

The apostle goes on to point out that the mind is a slave to God, but the flesh is enslaved to the law of sin. In the very next chapter, however, he points out how the Holy Spirit assists us in our weakness and frailty, making possible what human will cannot make possible at all.

For the Jewish community, keeping the law is not a simple matter, of course, but keeping the law is also not beyond human capacity— precisely because the Giver of the law has seen to that. See how the book of Deuteronomy addresses this question:

> Surely, this commandment that I am commanding you today is not too hard for you, nor is it too far away. . . . No, the word is very near to you; it is in your mouth and in your heart for you to observe. (Deut. 30:11, 14)

Perhaps the difference between Jewish and Christian perspectives is related to the remarkable demands of Jesus' words to his followers on the Sermon on the Mount: "Be perfect, therefore, as your heavenly Father is perfect." (Matt. 5:48)

The "Impossible Possibility"

In the Sermon on the Mount (Matt. 5–7), Jesus affirms and strengthens the demands of Torah. Another dimension, however, is added: Jesus insists that the promises of God to Israel's prophets and seers of a new day of righteousness, peace, and blessedness was already dawning. No one needed to wait any longer for some new, divine intervention: the kingdom of God was at hand (Mark 1:15). Again, the specific import of this declaration of Jesus has been debated through the centuries. It is still debated. In my judgment, it is the center of Jesus' message. Just as Israel's prophets called on the community to recognize that what God was bringing to earth—peace with righteousness, just rulers, a divine welcome for all the sick and troubled and despised of earth in the holy city, and the end of all violence and destruction— was sure to come, Jesus boldly declared that it had come. Israel's prophets called on the people to shape their lives then and there in the light of God's promises. See the call of Isaiah, "O house of Jacob, come, let us walk in the light of the LORD!" (Isa. 2:5), which follows upon Isaiah's vision of the march of the nations to Jerusalem, earth's center, where God's Torah was to be extended to all the nations.

These promises of God through Israel's prophets were a summons to action, a call to live *now* as citizens of a transformed city, a transformed earth. Jesus takes that message even farther: that quality of life is not only possible; it is God's gift here and now.

Jesus surely knew that Rome was still oppressing his people, that injustice flourished all around him, and that his followers were fallible human beings just as everyone else was. Still, he insisted, "Be perfect . . . as your heavenly Father is perfect" (Matt. 5:48). The call is to claim the power that God makes available to anticipate the complete, authentic, proper life that God has purposed from the beginning. Think what a judgment of God it is on a society that has it in its power to live more nearly in accord with God's just and peaceful rule on earth—but does not do so!

But consider what hope for the future underlies this belief in the rule of God that is even now, in our midst, being realized! And consider too the lure, the drawing power, of such visions of God's perfect rule on earth as one seeks now to follow God's path! When Jesus called the community to accept the truth that God did not need to do anything more than was already done in order to live in the at-hand divine kingdom, he was showing, I believe, how confident he was in the truth of those promises of Israel's prophets. We Christians have the right to believe, in my judgment, that he may have understood those promises even better than the prophets to whom the visions were disclosed!

And that is where the "impossible possibility" comes into focus. We Christians believe that, by the power of the Spirit present in the community of believers and in the hearts of individual members, we are living life in the kingdom of God here and now. Not perfectly, of course, for the drag of personal ambition and greed and fear and all the products of human unrest and anxiety plague us and draw us from the path laid out before us.

Christians through the centuries have developed and accepted some notion of what is called "original" sin. Following a false reading of Psalm 51, "Behold, I was shapen in iniquity; and in sin did my mother conceive me" (King James Version), many interpreters have connected the "first" sin of the first human pair in the garden as somehow transmitted through the generations by means of the sexual act. Such a notion is absurd scientifically, and it is not what the psalmist meant at all. Psalm 51:5 means, according to the psalmist, that there was never a time that the author can remember not being already bent toward the wrong. The New Revised Standard Version translates, correctly, "Indeed, I was born guilty, a sinner when my mother conceived me." This is a way of saying that the poet cannot wriggle out of the sin being confessed by claiming that it was a fluke, something not characteristic, for the psalmist's true self was not like that at all. On the contrary, the author says, this sinful person is who I am; God help me, I have to own up to the truth and make a true confession.

For me, "original" sin and "original" righteousness go together. They represent what the prior generation passes on to the current generation and what the current generation, in turn, will pass along to its successor generation. A vivid example from our own time is the effect of racism on our entire people. My generation has been blessed by enormous gains in interracial understanding and by concrete decline in the effects of racism on the majority population and the minority populations alike. But we know well, and sadly, that we are also passing along to the next generation much of the institutional racism and the personal racial prejudice that still has a firm hold on us.

We can thank God that progress takes place. I am convinced that, over time, the good outweighs the evil. It is hard to recognize the truth of that belief, since every gain made sharpens the mind and sensibilities to see dimensions of evil that we had not seen before. The result is that we find it hard to believe in progress.

In short, "original" sin means that flawed social and personal structure of evil into which every individual is born and which every social organization inherits along with the positive gifts of the prior generation.

The author of 2 Esdras 3–10 (not accepted as Scripture by most churches but one of the books of the Apocrypha that deserves to be more widely known) struggles to understand why God could not or did not find some way to arrange for the destructiveness of evil to be checked. An interpreting angel tries to distract Esdras (or Ezra, the Hebrew name) from worrying about the fate of sinners, urging him, rather, to fix his eye on the few righteous whom God will spare at the Last Judgment. Ezra cannot be distracted: How can God be content with the destruction of most of the population of earth because of the sin of Israel and of all nations? The author's answer comes in a vision of Zion/Jerusalem, being rebuilt with huge foundations, pointing to God's extraordinary love and mercy for the flawed creation. To my mind, this is a much better image of the world's future than the one so frequently drawn, say, in the popular "Left Behind" literature. Who wants to be taken up in such a world? or left behind? Like the Ezra of 2 Esdras, I cannot see how one can live with the anticipation that only a few of the righteous of earth are to survive divine judgment and wrath.

The wideness of God's mercy is marvelously expressed in a key text that seeks to portray the very inner being of God: Exodus 34:6–7, a text that is quoted in part in every type of Old Testament literature and is dealt with at length in 2 Esdras. Moses has gone back up the mountain to receive the text of the Ten Commandments once more, after the idolatry with the golden calf (chap. 32). God comes to Moses and pronounces this poetic description of just who God is and what the divine character actually is:

> "The LORD, the LORD,
> a God merciful and gracious,
> slow to anger,
> and abounding in steadfast love and faithfulness,
> keeping steadfast love for the thousandth generation,
> forgiving iniquity and transgression and sin,
> yet by no means clearing the guilty,
> but visiting the iniquity of the parents
> upon the children
> and the children's children,
> to the third and the fourth generation."

Through the centuries, this listing of what has been called God's attributes has loomed large in Jewish and Christian portrayals of the inner character of God. The author of 1 John sums it up well: "God is love" (1 John 4:8).

The Commandment to Love

Jewish and Christian Scripture commands that we love God and neighbor. Jesus puts the matter more strongly, "Love your enemies" (Matt. 5:44). The command to love means more than to show concern and respect for God and neighbor. The text from Deuteronomy 6, "Hear, O Israel: The LORD is our God, the LORD alone," continues with a demand to love God with all one's heart and soul and might (Deut. 6:4–5) Similarly, the command to love one's neighbor is speaking about an attitude and a commitment of the heart, for it begins, "You shall not take vengeance or bear a grudge against any of your people" (Lev. 19:18). Love of God and neighbor is unmistakably commanded of Israel and of the Christian community.

But can love be commanded? We saw above that God prohibits coveting, and that, we argued, is a matter of heart and will. The prohibitions of the Ten Commandments rightly infer love of God and neighbor, and this love is just as much a divine demand as are the prohibitions.

Of course, love is also a spontaneous act, a very personal disposition that changes our very character. Loving God and the neighbor, it seems, simply flows out of the inward recesses of the self into deeds of praise to God and deeds of love for our fellow human beings. One central outgrowth of love of God and neighbor is, as the Gospel of John says, keeping the commandments (John 14:15). Does it not follow, then, that keeping the commandments is itself an expression of our love for God and neighbor?

Small wonder, then, that Jesus proclaimed that the greatest of the commandments are love of God and neighbor (see Mark 12:28–34 and its parallels). If one wishes to have the Ten Commandments put in a positive form, there it is: Love God and love your neighbor.

Love God, Love God's Law

Israel's love for God is matched by love for Torah. Psalm 19 opens, "The heavens are telling the glory of God; and the firmament proclaims his handiwork." Without a sound, the world of God's creation sings God's praises, precisely by obeying God's laws governing their movements. The second part of this psalm describes the benefits of God's Torah: Torah revives the soul, makes the simple ones wise, rejoices the heart, enlightens the eyes, and endures forever. Its very taste on the tongue is like honey. Small wonder, then, that the author of Psalm 119 can exclaim, "Oh, how I love your law!" (Ps. 119:97).

Like God's wisdom, God's Torah is a precious reality, so intimately related to deity that its presence is almost equivalent to God's presence. To know the Law is to love the Law, and to know and love the Law is to know and love God. The author of Sirach 24 in the Apocrypha goes so far as to identify Woman Wisdom with Torah, both feminine counterparts to God in some sense. Jewish and Christian piety often have expressed this connection between loving God and loving God's ways. One popular Christian chorus uses another line from Psalm 119, "Thy word is a lamp unto my feet, and a light unto my path" (Ps. 119:105 KJV).

God's gift of Torah, then, is in two forms—negative and positive. Torah is entrusted to Israel in behalf of the whole world. Stated negatively, the Ten Commandments graciously guide the community away from acts and desires that will damage, if they do not destroy, the life in community that is God's gift and purpose for all. Stated positively, they all clearly coalesce in love and devotion to God that wells up from love and gratitude and spreads out to enrich and transform all of life. Torah was granted first to Israel, according to Scripture, but Torah is intended for all. What better example of that intention could we ask for than Isaiah's vision of the day when the nations would stream up to Jerusalem to receive God's Torah, recognizing on the journey that Torah means that weapons of warfare are worthless. Torah means peace with righteousness for the nations, and joy and delight for every heart (Isa. 2:2–4; see Mic. 4:1–4).

Questions for Discussion

1. What is wrong with the common adage "The Old Testament is a book of law; the New Testament is a book of grace"?
2. In what ways do the Ten Commandments enhance freedom?
3. Both Jewish and Christian Scripture command that we love God and neighbor. But can love be commanded? Is love a matter of the heart or the will?

7

Should We Post the Commandments in Public Places?

*S*ince I have written frequently about the Ten Commandments during the last forty-five years, I sometimes get asked to take a position on one of the "hot issues" of American public life: Should we post the Ten Commandments on the walls of our courtrooms and in other public places, or is such posting a violation of the antiestablishment clause of the Bill of Rights? At various times I have presented arguments for both positions, and I wish to do so here as well.

Several questions have to be answered in order for a reasonable conclusion to be drawn, in my judgment. We have to decide just what sort of document the Ten Commandments are. Are they dependent for their meaning on their religious importance for Jews and Christians, or might they have a moral and social value independent of their religious heritage? If they are a religious statement, may they still legitimately be posted because ours was in its founding a Christian land, and the founders intended that ours always be a Christian commonwealth? Are the Ten Commandments a policy statement rather than a set of laws, whether religious or secular, and therefore perhaps useful to the society whether or not treated as religious?

The evangelical scholar and preacher Tony Campolo once wrote a column against the posting of the Ten Commandments in which he made a special point: Are the Ten Commandments the very best part of biblical thought to be posted in public places? Why not the Golden Rule? or the Beatitudes? or the two "greatest commandments," according to Jesus—the love of God and neighbor? Why should we be so intent on having the Ten

Commandments on public school grounds or in our public buildings? Do they really sum up the best of the biblical heritage?

Tony Campolo has a point—if what society needed were the best of biblical verses to commend and memorize. The Ten Commandments, as I have sought to show above, have a distinct character, marvelously well outlining for individuals and groups critically important kinds of human behavior that will surely do harm and damage, if indeed they do not bring ruin on individuals and communities.

The Argument against Posting

The First Amendment to the U.S. Constitution opens with the following clause: "Congress shall make no law respecting an establishment of religion, or prohibiting the free exercise thereof." This carefully balanced, negatively framed statement is capable of many interpretations, as our history has shown. It clearly rules out two things: first, the amendment rules out legal identification of the United States as a Christian nation. Some states once identified one form of Christianity as the established religion of that state (Congregationalism in Connecticut, Anglicanism in Virginia, for example), but the new union of states was not to declare Christianity in any of its forms as the religion of the land.

Secondly, the new union of states was not to take legal steps to prohibit any citizen from practicing his or her religion freely. Apart from these fairly clear guidelines, many issues remained in doubt. Early in the history of the republic, one view gained prominence, indicated by the phrase "separation of church and state." Also early on, those states that had legally identified one form of Christianity as the established religion took steps to remove that identification. In order to avoid discrimination on the basis of religious belief or affiliation, individuals and groups began to encourage federal, state, and local governments to avoid all actions that might be understood to favor any particular religion or to deal prejudicially with any particular religion.

Long before the adoption of the First Amendment, religious dissenters to established Christianity in New England had protested and, under the leadership of Roger Williams and others, had established the principle of religious freedom as a hallmark of the New World. Adoption of the First Amendment owes much to their insistence that citizens must be free to worship God as they choose, or not to worship God if they so choose.

The government, however, was not indifferent to religion. Chaplains served in the armed forces and in the houses of Congress. The coinage and currency of the land testified to belief in God, and the courts administered oaths by reference to God and with the witness's hand placed on the Christian Bible. Such concessions to the majority religion of the citizens did not, however, extend to the specific use of federal funds in support of religious schools or clergy or congregations. Such practices were viewed with suspicion by "free church" Christians who had long been opposed to any governmental interference in their religious practices. Roger Williams' establishment of Rhode Island prior to the American Revolution was a major pointer of this way.

The establishment of a public school system brought changes. Many such schools opened the school day with religious acts such as the reading of Scripture, the singing of Christian (largely Protestant and evangelical) hymns, and Christian prayer. Such practices went unchallenged until the rapid increase of Roman Catholic and Jewish immigration brought challenges to the practice. By the twentieth century, agencies such as the American Civil Liberties Union (ACLU) formed to safeguard the separation of church and state. Separation of church and state has been a rallying cry for Baptists in America—until the last two decades, when Southern Baptist national leaders have completely reversed course and called for favored treatment of the majority religion, Christianity.

Gains Resulting from Strict Separation

The major gain produced by strict separation of church and state is not in doubt. Religion has been required to be self-supporting and self-regulating, with the result that in no other land (until recent years in some third-world lands) has Christianity flourished as it has in the United States and Canada. Those who accept the truth and power of their religious commitment have been required to support their community's leaders and missions—and they have done so with remarkable generosity. Income from all U.S. Christian church contributions in 2003 totaled more than thirty-two billion dollars.[1]

Religious groups in North America established private schools, colleges, hospitals, orphanages, and many other institutions as a direct result of the separation of church and state. Over the centuries, many of these institutions have come to be supported in part by state and federal funds. This network of religious institutions continues to contribute immensely to the education, health, and general welfare of the society even as the institutions continue to pursue their particular religious commitments.

Another gain, not as widely recognized as it should be, is the spread of teaching about religion in schools and colleges of North America and of other lands as well. The many Christian colleges of North America for many decades taught Christianity, and their particular brand thereof, to their students and also supported their church bodies through trained leaders. Naturally enough, the Christian theological schools created for the training of Christian clergy did their work for their church bodies. More and more, however, these theological schools also joined in the work of "secular" programs in religion to enable the populace to understand the contributions of religious beliefs and understandings for the society as a whole. Thus, society had the benefit of informed teaching about religion on the part of flourishing religious communities that held to their distinctive beliefs and teachings while respecting the views of those who differed from them. Religious tolerance was a direct outgrowth of the separation of church and state.

The effect of religious tolerance on biblical and theological scholarship has been enormous. The Society of Biblical Literature, founded in New York City in 1880, for many decades carefully left aside any discussion of controversial political or social questions. It could not, of course, leave aside entirely the question of the Bible's authority and issues of the canon. By severely concentrating on history and literature, however, the Society was able to maintain good relations with most religious groups in North America, even the most theologically conservative, including those who considered the Bible as the inerrant, infallible Word of God. That wholesome situation continues to this day, even though members of the Society today feel at greater liberty to address issues of critical importance to public life and public morals, including such issues as homosexuality, abortion, war and peace, poverty and riches, and even the establishment of religion.

America's Religious Pluralism

As matters turned out, the First Amendment proved to be exactly what the United States needed in order to deal with the flood of immigrants who brought enormous variety to the religious world of the states, both to the first thirteen states and to each of the new states in turn. Virtually every form of Christianity was soon represented in the United States, plus the several forms of Judaism, with Islam and many other religions to follow, including Hinduism, Buddhism, Confucianism, Taoism, and Shinto. Native American religions also, after having suffered immeasurable damage during the period of settlement in the West, now claim an appropriate place in public life and culture.

The Argument for Posting

One of the major failures of my generation of specialists in religion is, I believe, our inability to find a suitable curriculum for offering instruction in religion in our public schools. Even strict application of the doctrine of separation of church and state does not, of course, entirely rule out such instruction *about* religion. What is ruled out is the favoring of one religion over others. Only in recent decades in the United States have groups and institutions sought to meet this need. The results have not come without great difficulty. One popular program has been shown to be far from impartial: offered as objective scholarship, it clearly and throughout favors one form of evangelical Christianity. Other programs are better, and the day may be near when secondary schools in the United States can include, with confidence that indoctrination is not likely, courses on, for example, the history and literature of the Jewish and Christian Bibles, or the history and literature of the various world religions.

But what of the Ten Commandments? Surely, one might argue, the posting of the Ten Commandments represents an effort to impose a piece of Jewish and Christian religious belief on the entire population and, in addition, a set of moral guidelines for all to follow!

Not necessarily. One of the great difficulties with a strict enforcement of the separation of church and state is that the entire public school population is being denied a full presentation of its historical and cultural heritage. The social, cultural, and literary heritage of a society invariably includes religion, but a strict application of the doctrine of the separation of church and state has led to religion's being excluded from most public school classrooms. Or, rather, the major religious traditions of the United States—Judaism and Christianity—tend to be excluded. It has been possible to present in social studies classes a considerable perspective on the religions of the world other than those two. Might it not be entirely appropriate to have the Ten Commandments, clearly a significant part of that cultural heritage, displayed in public places?

As noted above, it all depends on just how one understands the nature and character of the Ten Commandments. As I have sought to show in earlier chapters, the commandments provide a set of guidelines that offer moral guidance quite apart from their religious/theological setting. Even the first three commandments do more than offer divine commands; they make general points about the nature of the world and of the relations of human beings to that world. The world has a unitary character: it is *one world*, with all its parts interrelated and blessed. Human beings have special responsibility for the care of the world, and the nonhuman part of the world has its own part to play in sustaining all life.

For the Bible, keeping the commandments is not only a divine command. It is also sensible, prudent, and morally right. Some biblical scholars are convinced that ancient Israel understood the whole of the Law, including the summary of the Law found in the Ten Commandments, to be rooted in the very structure of the creation.[2] The Law, in this view, applies to the whole of the creation—all human beings, and even the nonhuman parts of the creation. In the creation story of Genesis 1 this point is made clear: earth has its own part in creation (Gen. 1:11, 24–25), and so do the sun and moon and stars (vv. 16–18), the seas (v. 20), and the creatures of sea and sky (vv. 21–22). Of course, this remains a biblical-theological understanding, but it entitles modern interpreters to point out that a secular understanding of this view of the laws of nature is consistent with a theological view. Once again, the argument for posting the commandments would seem not to depend on their Jewish and Christian origins and character.

Civil Religion

In two federal district court cases in which I have participated as a so-called "expert witness," I have argued that the U.S. government should let stand certain plaques with abbreviated forms of the Ten Commandments because of their wide usefulness in presenting time-tested moral guidelines for a secular society. Jewish and Christian observers will, of course, see the commandments as a part of their theological tradition and honor them in that way. Those who do not share Jewish or Christian religious beliefs can and, I believe, should recognize their value for the society as a whole.

Religion, I argued, works that way in all societies. There are those who hold firmly (sometimes fanatically, sadly) to the religious beliefs as the utter and unqualified truth of life. Others, usually the majority, find the faith (into which they probably were introduced as children) to be useful, valuable, and true, and are glad to identify themselves with that religion, support it, and instill its views and beliefs in the lives of their children. Still others find the religion morally useful, care little about its special doctrines and practices, but claim it for its benefits to them and to the larger society.

Others, of course, reject Judaism and Christianity, and indeed may consider them harmful to society. Even for such persons, the Ten Commandments offer excellent moral guidance and should not be found offensive. What is offensive is the effort to press one's own religion on others who do not wish to have this pressure. True religious tolerance, I argued, recognizes that documents such as the Ten Commandments can serve many purposes for many groups of people. Only one of those groups is fully served when the posting of the Ten Commandments is prohibited: the strict separationists who want to be sure that no group is given offense by such posting. Others of course may take offense at the prominence given these materials from Jewish and Christian tradition, but the issue is, do they really need to do so? Might the objections of some, at least, among those who oppose posting be misplaced?

I am not saying, of course, that the majority position in a given land has a right to override all objections by minorities. Such a view does not take with sufficient seriousness the rights of minorities in a society.

If the posting of the Ten Commandments actually forced a specific religious viewpoint on the community, intrusively pressing that religious outlook on persons who might be harmed by the pressure, that would be sufficient reason for not posting.

Examples abound that would be offenses against the First Amendment. Let us look at a few and see if they do not differ in important ways from the posting of the Ten Commandments. But first, let me mention an example of nonoffensive presentation of the biblical heritage. I recall the story told by a Jewish colleague at Vanderbilt Divinity School years ago about a course on "The Bible as Literature" in the high school in which the Jewish scholar's children were enrolled. The teacher shared the Jewish and Christian heritages out of the Bible with such thoughtfulness, open-mindedness, and literary and religious sensitivity, said my colleague, that his children benefited greatly, and he and his wife were delighted with the result. My colleague often spoke of this experience in order to affirm that there are ways to present Judaism and Christianity in secondary-school education that do not at all violate the spirit and intention of the First Amendment.

Examples of other kinds abound. I was asked recently to support the application of a former colleague who had been urged to apply for an opening to teach a Bible course in a North Carolina high school. He was given a copy of the textbook that was to be used, a work touted as an objective presentation of the Jewish and Christian biblical heritages. He found that it was far from objective, being designed to establish the historicity of the biblical accounts of creation, flood, and the like, and generally written to demonstrate the accuracy of fundamentalist biblical claims. He thought that he might be able to do the course, even so, working around some of the problems presented by the textbook. But shortly after he had been invited to teach the class, the invitation was withdrawn, and the school officials found another (safe?) teacher.

More directly to the point are notable examples of efforts to post the Ten Commandments in massive form in courthouses or on school grounds, with the unmistakable intention of pressing the claims of those who have set out to rewrite the history of the founding of the United States republic—claiming that the founders clearly intended to establish the United States as a Christian nation. This claim, supported by a flood of media claims pouring over us for the last decade, is clearly wrong, as many evangelical historians of American religious thought acknowledge.[3] Of course I agree with Mark Noll: the founders were deeply committed to the principle of religious liberty and had no intention whatever of establishing a Christian commonwealth. The First Amendment makes that unmistakably clear. Any acceptable rationale for posting the Ten Commandments in public places must surely exclude any such false notion.

In one of the federal district court cases in which I was involved, the county officers who were quizzed by the attorneys for the plaintiff—a man who was convinced that the presence of Lady Justice, pictured behind the judge's bench in the county courthouse with an abridgment of the Ten Commandments on two plaques surrounding Lady Justice, had prejudiced his case before the judge—all offered testimony that was the opposite of my testimony. For the officers of the county, the plaques and Lady Justice should remain precisely because ours is a Christian country and the presence of replicas of the Ten Commandments on a courthouse wall rightly affirms that truth.

The argument that I have sought to make is simple. The Ten Commandments are a critical part of ancient jurisprudence. They can be understood, and often are so understood, as moral guidelines for the society, stated in primarily negative form, assisting a society with basic moral guidance. Whether one believes that these moral guidelines are a part of natural law, and thus built into the very structure of human society, or considers them simply (!) the fruit of human experience and reflection, or indeed considers them a part of divine revelation to ancient Israel, accepted and reaffirmed by the Founder of Christianity, the Ten Commandments can serve a society well. They alert a society to forms of human conduct that are to be avoided at all cost (eight of the commandments) or to be faithfully observed (Sabbath observance and the honoring of parents). They require interpretation by every community that accepts them, but they boldly stand as guides to moral behavior useful to all societies and their individual members.

Perhaps I should be content to maintain that in those instances in which the Ten Commandments, in whole or in part, have found a place on our public buildings we should gratefully acknowledge the wisdom of those responsible for their placement and leave them intact. Portions of the Ten Commandments are located along the upper walls of the main room of the U.S. Supreme Court Building in Washington. Surely, they should not be removed. But those who believe, as I do, that a case can be made for their being posted more widely surely have the burden of proof that such posting is thoroughly consistent with both features of the First Amendment on religious liberty: they do not in any way seek to establish Christianity or any religion as the religion of this republic, and their posting is simply an instance of our claiming the right of "free exercise" of our religious understandings. In my judgment, such a posting would not be the camel's nose under the tent that would overthrow the respected doctrine of separation of church and state. We owe our fellow citizens and ourselves and our families all the guidance we can gain from our religious heritages, including the moral guidance to be gained from all of the world's religious traditions and teachings.

Can These Views Be Reconciled?

What can we conclude about these two alternatives? Is there some position or understanding that might prove satisfactory to both groups? Perhaps we must admit at the outset that the conflict is beyond resolution for some persons and groups. Surely, however, most of us recognize that the First Amendment is attempting precisely to protect the rights of those who insist on the freedom to worship God as they see fit while also protecting the rights of citizens who do not wish to have any form of religion imposed on them or to have their government supporting any religious community or movement. It then becomes a judgment question whether the presence of the Ten Commandments in public places seems likely to impose a religious statement on those who would be adversely affected by that posting. Surely there is a difference between the creation of a massive statue of Moses holding the Ten Commandments placed prominently in a public building or on public grounds and a frieze on a courthouse wall that depicts the Roman deity Justitia and plaques of the Ten Commandments on either side of her. The first shouts out the claim that ours is a Christian nation and one will receive Christian justice in this courthouse. The other points to historic efforts to live by the rule of law, admittedly drawing prominently on texts that are religiously important for Jews and Christians, but doing so modestly and without fanfare.

Actually, as we all know, the major battle is not over the posting of the Ten Commandments. The battle is to determine whether a vocal and well-organized religious minority will succeed in convincing the majority that all the institutions of U.S. government should give prominence and place of preference to a particular form of Christianity. This group wishes to assure that the science curriculum presents the findings of the sciences in a form congenial to their Christian belief. The group wants federal and state support for schools, federal and state programs that protect and affirm its understandings of when human life begins and ends, and legislators and judges who share their outlook. Nothing less than a Christian America, defined in their way, will suffice.

Nonetheless, the posting of the Ten Commandments is an important issue that needs to be thought through. Both the arguments for not posting them and the arguments for posting them have cogency, in my judgment. Perhaps in situations like this, we should place the burden of argument for removing such postings as already exist squarely on those who say, "Do not post." And perhaps we should correspondingly place the burden of argument for new postings squarely on those who say, "Post." In other words, let's keep the postings we have but be wary of additional ones.

Questions for Discussion

1. What arguments can you identify against posting the Ten Commandments?
2. What arguments can you identify in favor of posting the Ten Commandments?
3. What middle ground, if any, do you see between these two alternatives?

Notes

Chapter 1: Law Is a Gift of God

1. The third commandment says that the LORD will not consider an offender of the commandment to be without guilt, but it does not prescribe any punishment.

Chapter 2: God Is One

1. As we noted above, the numbering of the commandments is quite varied among the religious communities. Since the Jewish community includes Exod. 20:2 as a part of the first commandment, that verse belongs here as well. Some Christian communities combine the first and the second commandments as listed above. The content of the commandments is always the same—only the numbering differs.

Chapter 4: Protecting Life and Marriage

1. The *New English Bible*; the *Revised English Bible*; the *New King James Version*; the *New International Version*; the *Tanakh*—Jewish Publication Society Bible; the *New Revised Standard Version*, and many other recent translations translate "murder." The *Jerusalem Bible* and the *New Jerusalem Bible*, along with the *New American Translation*, both Roman Catholic translations, retain "kill."
2. See Wilma Ann Bailey, *You Shall Not Kill or You Shall Not Murder? The Assault on a Biblical Text* (Collegeville, MN: Liturgical Press, 2005).

Chapter 5: Ensuring Wholesome Life in Community

1. See the lengthy treatment by Marvin L. Chaney, "Coveting Your Neighbor's House in Social Context," in *The Ten*

Commandments: The Reciprocity of Faithfulness, ed. William P. Brown (Louisville, KY: Westminster John Knox Press, 2004), 302–17. Chaney (wrongly, I believe) thinks that a commandment against coveting almost inevitably upholds the status quo and serves the ends of the haves against the have-nots. I believe the opposite.

Chapter 6: Keeping the Commandments

1. See chapter 7 of Job for a parody of the glorious hymn in praise of God's creation of humankind in Psalm 8.

Chapter 7: Should We Post the Commandments in Public Places?

1. See "Summary Statistics of Church Finances," in *Yearbook of American & Canadian Churches 2005,* ed. Eileen W. Lindner. National Council of the Churches of Christ in the U.S.A. (Nashville: Abingdon Press, 2005), 387.
2. See the lengthy treatment by Terence E. Fretheim, *God and World in the Old Testament* (Nashville: Abingdon Press, 2005).
3. See the fine book by Mark A. Noll, *A History of Christianity in the United States and Canada* (Grand Rapids: Wm. B. Eerdmans Publishing Co., 1992), 132–36.

Further Reading

Barclay, William. *The Ten Commandments*. Louisville, KY: Westminster John Knox Press, 1998.

Brown, William P., ed. *The Ten Commandments: The Reciprocity of Faithfulness*. Louisville, KY: Westminster John Knox Press, 2004.

Harrelson, Walter J. *The Ten Commandments and Human Rights*. Rev. ed. Macon, GA: Mercer University Press, 1997.

Hauerwas, Stanley M., and William H. Willimon. *The Truth About God: The Ten Commandments in Christian Life*. Nashville: Abingdon Press, 1999.

Smedes, Lewis B. *Mere Morality: What God Expects from Ordinary People*. Grand Rapids: Wm. B. Eerdmans Publishing Co., 1983.